The AIA Guide to Columbus

The AIA Guide to Columbus

Jeffrey T. Darbee and Nancy A. Recchie
for the
Columbus Architecture Foundation
and
AIA Columbus
A Chapter of the American Institute of Architects

Preface by the Honorable Michael B. Coleman
Mayor, City of Columbus

OHIO UNIVERSITY PRESS • ATHENS, OHIO

Ohio University Press, Athens, Ohio 45701
www.ohio.edu/oupress

Printed in China

Photo Credits

Richard K. Loesch: 1-1a, 3-6, 6-1, 15-1, 15-5

Feinknopf Photography: front cover, 1-1b, 1-6, 1-8, 1-12, 1-14, 2-5, 2-8, 2-10, 3-2b, 3-5, 4-4, 4-7b, 4-8b, 4-9, 4-16b, 5-6b, 5-8, 5-9, 5-18a, 5-18b, 6-4, 6-9, 7-1a, 7-5, 7-7, 7-9a. 7-10, 7-11a, 7-11b, 8-1, 8-2, 9-2, 11-3, 12-4, 12-6, 12-9, 12-10, 12-11, 12-12, 12-13, 12-14, 12-15, 12-17a, 12-17b, 12-17c, 14-1, 14-4, 14-9, 14-11, 14-12, 14-13, 14-14, 15-6, 16-3, 16-4, 16-6, 16-7, 17-1a, 18-1, 18-4, 21-3, 22-3, 22-4

Robert D. Loversidge, Jr.: 1-1c, 1-11b, 3-1, 4-2, 4-8a, 4-14, 5-16, 5-17a, 5-17b, 6-3, 7-8, 11-2, 14-7b, 15-2, 15-3, 17-1b, 18-2b, 18-5, 18-6, 19-2, 21-4, 22-1b

Donald Olshavsky: 1-2, 1-3, 1-4, 1-5, 1-7, 1-9, 1-10a, 1-10b, 1-11a, 1-13, 1-15, 2-1, 2-2, 2-3, 2-4, 2-6, 2-7, 2-9, 3-2a, 3-3, 3-4, 4-1, 4-3, 4-5, 4-6a, 4-7a, 4-10, 4-11, 4-12, 4-13, 4-16a, 5-1,5-2, 5-3, 5-4, 5-5, 5-6a, 5-7, 5-10, 5-11, 5-12, 5-13, 5-14, 5-15, 6-2, 6-5, 6-6, 6-7, 6-8, 6-10, 7-1b, 7-2, 7-3, 7-4, 7-6, 8-3, 9-1, 11-1, 12-2, 12-3, 12-5, 12-8, 12-16, 12-18, 13-1, 14-2, 14-3, 14-6, 14-7a, 14-8, 14-10, 15-4, 15-7, 15-8, 16-1, 16-2, 16-5, 16-8, 17-2, 17-3, 18-2a, 18-3, 19-1, 20-1, 20-2, 21-5, 22-1a, 22-2, 22-5, 22-6

George C. Anderson, Emery Photography: 4-6b

John F. Hedge: 4-15

Ellen Puckett Photography: 7-9b

The Ohio State University: 12-1

Tim Hursley: 12-7

Brian M. Dieterle: 14-9a

Richard Pontius: 21-1a, 21-b

Photos by owners: 10-1, 13-2, 13-3, 14-5, 21-2

Ohio University Press books are printed on acid-free paper ∞ ™

15 14 13 12 11 10 09 08 5 4 3 2 1

Library of Congress Cataloging-in-Publication Data

Darbee, Jeffrey T.
The AIA guide to Columbus / Jeffrey T. Darbee and Nancy A. Recchie for the Columbus Architecture Foundation and AIA Columbus, a chapter of the American Institute of Architects ; preface by the Honorable Michael B. Coleman.
p. cm.
Includes index.
ISBN-13: 978-0-8214-1684-6 (hc : alk. paper)
ISBN-10: 0-8214-1684-7 (hc : alk. paper)
ISBN-13: 978-0-8214-1685-3 (pb : alk. paper)
ISBN-10: 0-8214-1685-5 (pb : alk. paper)
1. Architecture—Ohio—Columbus—Guidebooks. 2. Columbus (Ohio)—Buildings, structures, etc.—Guidebooks. 3. Columbus (Ohio)—Guidebooks. I. Title: American Institute of Architects guide to Columbus. II. Title: Guide to Columbus. III. Recchie, Nancy A. IV. Columbus Architecture Foundation (Columbus, Ohio) V. American Institute of Architects. Columbus Chapter (Columbus, Ohio) VI. Title.
NA735.C65D37 2007
720.9771'57—dc22

2007030422

Contents

Gems

Dedicated to

Elliot Leonard Whitaker, FAIA

1910–1998

Foreword

Since its founding in 1812, Columbus, the largest city in Ohio, has been home to many impressive architectural landmarks. *The AIA Guide to Columbus,* written by Jeffrey Darbee and Nancy Recchie and produced by the Columbus Architecture Foundation, highlights the significant buildings and neighborhoods in the Columbus metropolitan area, with an emphasis on the downtown. Blending architectural interest with historic significance, this book documents about 160 of our most significant buildings and sites.

The Columbus Architecture Foundation is a not-for-profit charitable organization that has been affiliated with AIA Columbus, the local chapter of the American Institute of Architects, for more than thirty years, with the joint missions of educational outreach and advocacy for high-quality design of the built environment. Our first book project, *Architecture: Columbus,* published in 1976, is considered to be the standard reference book about Columbus architecture. This new guide, in the works for about ten years, updates the information and provides a portable, accessible guide to the city's rich architectural mix. Other Foundation activities include the establishment of an architectural repository and archives at the Ohio Historical Society.

CAF owes a special debt of gratitude to Jane McMaster, who chaired our book committee; to Rich Pontius, AIA, for pitching the idea in the first place and for agreeing to do whatever was needed; to Rob Livesey, FAIA, for perseverance and editing; and to the late Elliot Whitaker, FAIA, for encouragement. We are also grateful to David Sanders and the Ohio University Press.

The American Institute of Architects was founded 150 years ago to "promote the scientific and practical perfection of its members" and "elevate the standing of the profession." Today the AIA has over 75,000 members, and it provides guidance, service, and standards to architects around the world. The AIA continues to strive for quality, consistency, and safety in the built environment and to serve as the voice of architecture. AIA Columbus was founded in 1913 and serves members in a thirty-county area.

Robert D. Loversidge, Jr., FAIA
Chair, Columbus Architecture Foundation

Preface

As the famous English prime minister and statesman Winston Churchill once said, "We shape our buildings and thereafter they shape us." We appreciate the work of the Columbus Architecture Foundation and the Columbus Chapter of the American Institute of Architects in producing this detailed guidebook to the great buildings of our city. I call Columbus "America's twenty-first-century city," and an integral part of our success lies in the mix of historic and modern architecture found throughout our community.

From the Harrison House to the State house to the new buildings on the Ohio State campus, this guide details important structures from all eras in our city's history.

I am pleased that the guide includes selections from our downtown, which is growing today with new life and energy to be everybody's neighborhood. Downtown is the social and economic heart of our region, and the place where the best of Columbus comes together, with fabulous architecture, an expansive riverfront, and extraordinary arts, sports, and entertainment venues.

As we attract new jobs and residents to Columbus, the built environment plays an important role in encouraging businesses to locate here, and in recruiting individuals to fill the jobs. This guidebook will provide a useful resource for local businesses, students, and those passionate about the diversity and quality of our unique local architecture heritage.

The Honorable Michael B. Coleman
Mayor, City of Columbus

Acknowledgments

COLUMBUS ARCHITECTURE FOUNDATION BOOK COMMITTEE

Jane McMaster, Chair
Robert S. Livesey, FAIA
Robert D. Loversidge, Jr., FAIA
Rich Pontius, AIA

COLUMBUS ARCHITECTURE FOUNDATION FUNDRAISING COMMITTEE

Chris Bendinelli, AIA, Chair
Robert D. Loversidge, Jr., FAIA

CURRENT COLUMBUS ARCHITECTURE FOUNDATION BOARD MEMBERS

Chris A. Bendinelli, AIA
David Wm. T. Carroll
Ed Lentz
Robert S. Livesey, FAIA
Robert D. Loversidge, Jr., FAIA, Chairman
Jane McMaster
Rich Pontius, AIA
John P. Schooley, FAIA
Diane Deane, ex officio

PHOTOGRAPHY

Donald Olshavsky
Brad Feinknopf, Feinknopf Photography
Richard K. Loesch, Cam-Tech Photography
Others as noted

MAPS

Orbit Design, Columbus, Ohio

During the long gestation period of this book, the Book Committee has worked hard to bring the project to completion. As chair, Jane McMaster coordinated production. She also wrote several grant proposals to help with funding, worked with one of the principal photographers, and served as liaison with the publisher. Rob Livesey worked on selecting buildings for the book and lent his expertise in editing as well as fundraising. Bob Loversidge chaired the early fundraising effort and continues on the committee, which is currently led by Chris Bendinelli. Bob also coordinated the final draft of the book, worked on the final version of the maps, took photographs, and served as liaison with the authors and the graphic design firm. Rich Pontius worked on selecting newer buildings for inclusion in the book, and he and Jane McMaster visited each one to evaluate its importance. He worked on several early drafts of the book, organizing the text and contributing to early versions of the maps, and he also created the index and compiled the glossary with Jane McMaster and Judith Kitchen.

Special Thanks

Reverend Robert L. Alexander; Mick Ball; Jim Barbee; Kay Benton; Sunny Bright; Richard Buchsieb; Michelle Buemi; Pastor Gary Chorpenning; David Carroll; Diane Cole; Tom Converse; Herb Cook; Mike Curtin; Jeff Darbee; Diane Deane; Don DeVere; Pastor Bob Duckens; Georgia Ehlers; Mark Feinknopf; Patsy L. Frost; Kenneth A. Gamble; Paul E. Goggin; Dellas H. Harder; Robert E. Hipp; David C. Hughes; Henry Hunker; Jeff Johns; Jay Kauh; Judith Kitchen; Amy Kobe; Ed Lentz; Richard K. Loesch; Sherie Lucas; Dixie Sayre Miller; Richard Miller; Rebecca Moore; Noverre Musson; Traci Parks; David Pierce; Ken Pierce; Barbara Powers; John Reagan; Cleve Ricksecker; Tim Rini; Reverend James D. Schimmel; James Schimmer; John P. Schooley; Msgr. Mario Serraglio; Society for Design Administration; Elliot L. Whitaker; Bill Wolfe; Paul E. Young, Jr.

Donors

BENEFACTORS

Columbus Chapter of the American Institute of Architects; Brad Feinknopf; Andrew W. Van Houten

PATRONS

DesignGroup; Greater Columbus Arts Council; Jones-Stuckey Ltd., Inc.; Messer Construction Company; Moody•Nolan, Inc.; MSI; NBBJ; Ohio Arts Council; RP Hughes Architects, Inc.; Schooley Caldwell Associates; Wolfe Associates

SPONSORS

Chris and Linda Bendinelli; *Columbus Dispatch;* Hamilton Parker; Junior League of Columbus; KPMG-Columbus; Jane and Robert McMaster; Dixie Sayre Miller; Dixie Sayre Miller Fund of the Columbus Foundation; Stone Centers, Inc.

CONTRIBUTORS

Baker Henning Productions; Dan A. Carmichael; Columbus Coal & Lime Co.; *Columbus Dispatch;* Georgia Ehlers; Mark G. Feinknopf; Geotechnical Consultants, Inc.; Jeffrey L. Glavan; Hanlin Industries Corp.; Dellas H. Harder; Industrial First, Inc.; Jezerinac Engineering; Kabil Associates; James L. Keyes; Ed Lentz; Lantz Jones Nebraska; Robert and Diana Livesey; Robert D. Loversidge, Jr.; Maddox-NBD Architecture; Matthews Click Bauman, Inc.; Meacham and Apel; John Reagan Architects; John P. Schooley; Trott Architects, Inc.; URS Consultants; Elliot L. Whitaker

FRIENDS

Patrick A. Burns; Robert L. Caldwell; David Carroll; Louis Cowan; Gandee and Associates; Jean P. Gordon; Robert P. Grinch; Donald R. Hoover; Dietmar Knodt; Lincoln Construction; McMullen Engineering Co., Inc.; SEM Partners; Joseph W. Sullivan; Wandel & Schnell Architects, Inc.; Paul E. Young, Jr.

AIA

AIA Columbus

GCAC
GREATER COLUMBUS ARTS COUNCIL

Ohio Arts Council

JUNIOR LEAGUE OF COLUMBUS
Women building better communities

How to Use This Guide

The *AIA Guide to Columbus* was written for two purposes: as a hands-on companion for visiting the capital city's rich architectural resources in person, and as a quick, factual reference guide to the architecture of Columbus.

The guide is organized into chapters showing buildings located within specific geographical areas within the downtown innerbelt, as well as chapters showing buildings that are grouped in a unique neighborhood or suburb. A separate chapter is devoted to the architecture of the Ohio State University, and the last chapter includes a collection of noteworthy "gems" located at various far-reaching corners of the city. Maps are included to assist with the design of walking or driving tours.

Each entry includes the name of the building or location, street address, date of completion, architect, and architectural style. Other significant additions and renovations are also noted. Entries that have been recognized as historic structures or have been recognized by professional societies are designated as follows:

NHL	National Historic Landmark
NR	National Register of Historic Places
CR	Columbus Register of Historic Properties
AIAC	Honor Award by the American Institute of Architects, Columbus Chapter
AIAO	Honor Award by the American Institute of Architects, Ohio Chapter
AIA	Honor Award by the American Institute of Architects
CLF	James B. Recchie Award by the Columbus Landmarks Foundation

At the conclusion of the guide are a glossary of architectural terms used in the book and an index cross-referencing building names, architects, and other notables. To learn more about the architectural styles referenced in the guide, we recommend obtaining a companion book entitled *What Style Is It?* published by the Preservation Press of the National Trust for Historic Preservation.

Private Houses

A few private houses are included in the guide. Please respect the homeowner's privacy. Do not trespass; most of the guide entries are visible from public streets.

Rich Pontius, AIA

Introduction

Columbus Development History

Ohio's capital city began not as a pioneer settlement but rather as a speculative investment. When Columbus was founded, the area around it was largely wilderness. A small community on the west bank of the Scioto River, known as Franklinton, had been established in 1797 by Lucas Sullivant, a federal government surveyor. The high land to the east of the river, however, remained in forest.

Ohio statehood came in 1803. With a permanent capital not yet selected, the state legislature met at Chillicothe until 1810, in Zanesville between 1810 and 1812, and then again in Chillicothe.

In 1812, the state sought proposals for a permanent capital from communities within forty miles of Ohio's geographic center. Four Franklinton land owners who had acquired title to the "High Banks Opposite Franklinton at the Forks of the Scioto" submitted a proposal that offered ten acres of land as a new site for a statehouse, ten acres for a penitentiary, and construction of public buildings not to exceed $50,000 in cost. The state accepted and Columbus was born.

The new seat of government had several north-south streets (Water, Front, High, and Third among others) and its northern and southern limits were what today are Nationwide Boulevard and Livingston Avenue. For many years, the new town had a frontier quality; tree stumps made passage along the streets difficult.

By 1815, as agreed, the Capital proprietors had funded the construction of a two-story brick statehouse with bell tower and an adjacent state office building at the southwest corner of today's Capitol Square at State and High streets. The population that year was about seven hundred. Travel to and from Columbus remained difficult, and growth was correspondingly slow, until the National Road and the Ohio and Erie Canal's Columbus Feeder reached the town in the early 1830s. These routes of commerce, imperfect though they were (the canal, for example, was closed by ice for several months each year), spurred growth and development, and the population surged to some 18,000 by 1850.

A line drawing looking down High Street from Broad in 1846 shows a small town encircling Capitol Square. Houses and one-story shops are interrupted by occasional churches and the multistory mass of the first of three Neil House hotels.

The first railroad reached Columbus in 1850, and by the mid-1850s the developed part of the city consisted of much of the area within today's Innerbelt Freeway. Residential development was concentrated around Capitol Square and throughout the immediate area, as well as along East Broad and East Town streets, where the wealthier citizens built. Most of the great mansions close to the downtown are gone now, but a hint of what once was here can be seen at the Columbus Club at Broad and Fourth streets and at the Kelton and Snowden-Gray houses on Town Street. The Town Street mansions are now museums and open to the public.

In the "Alte Sud Ende" (Old South End), the growing German population settled in what would become today's German Village. An Irish Village that was coming into being in the North End near the train station would eventually be swallowed up by railyards, but the quaint brick architecture of German Village—as American as it is German—is a remarkable preservation success story.

Within forty years, the city's rail network was composed of some fifteen lines connecting Columbus to all points of the compass. The state canal system went into permanent decline during this time and was abandoned early in the twentieth century. The National Road was turned over to the states through which it ran and would not thrive again until the Good Roads movement emerged in the era just before and after World War I.

Clearly, rail transportation was the wave of the future. Columbus railroads provided access to coalfields and other mineral supplies south of the city and were a reliable means of receiving other raw materials and shipping finished goods. Although the city never became a major industrial center comparable to Cleveland or Cincinnati, it was home to many different manufacturing enterprises, including makers of carriages, wagons, boots, shoes, foundry products, coal mining machinery, paint, glass, beer, and farm implements. Passenger trains on all the city's rail routes made travel throughout Ohio and beyond an easy matter.

By 1870, just over six square miles of land had been added to the city; by 1880, the urban area of Columbus was twenty-four square miles and extended about six miles north to south and about four miles east to west. The population of the city had grown to 88,000 in 1890, about a third of it of German heritage.

In addition to the factories that made all of the goods mentioned above, new office buildings using cast iron as well as stone and brick were rising three, four, and even five stories above downtown streets. Some, such as P. W. Huntington's bank at Broad and High, looked like castles. Others, such as Trinity Episcopal Church and the Hayden Bank Building on Broad Street, were even larger and more substantial.

But overshadowing them all was the Greek Revival Statehouse in the center of Capitol Square. When it was begun in 1839 to replace the original brick building, the original estimate was that the Statehouse would take two years to build and cost $200,000. In the end it took twenty-two years to build and cost $2,200,000. However, when it was done, it was one of America's great buildings. Recently renovated, it still is.

Within the city, a growing network of streetcar lines encouraged continued development outward from Capitol Square. Pulled by horses for their first thirty years, the streetcars were fully electrified by 1890 and were able to travel even farther. They created the "streetcar suburbs" of the early twentieth century, neighborhoods several miles from the center of town where people could live close to a streetcar line and have a reasonable commute to work. We can still see these neighborhoods in every direction from downtown. The houses—many of them quite large—sit close to one another. The newly emerging middle class in Columbus did not drive to work. People walked to the corner and took the streetcar downtown to where most of the city's jobs, shops, and entertainment were located. In the suburbs one found schools, churches, and the great parks, of which Goodale, Schiller, and Franklin were the largest.

At the turn of the twentieth century, Columbus had nearly 126,000 residents and was known as a center of government, insurance, and manufacturing. It was also an education center. Capital University, established in 1850, was the town's first college, but it would not be the last. By 1900, Columbus was home to what would eventually become Ohio Dominican University and Franklin University as well as the Ohio Agricultural and Mechanical College, now known as the Ohio State University.

Columbus had a thriving downtown business district and well-built substantial neighborhoods that began at the very edge of downtown and extended for several miles along the main east-west and north-south thoroughfares. The urban area, about ten miles from north to south and eight miles from east to west, was in the form of an irregular cross, the axes formed by Broad and High Streets.

Early in the twentieth century, the automobile became the primary force shaping the development of Columbus, an effect that accelerated as time went on. As people relied more on the auto and less on the streetcar lines, new areas became built up and the cross shape of the city began to fill in and spread out into a more circular form. Auto-dependent suburbs such as Bexley, Upper Arlington, and Grandview Heights began to grow and to develop their own commercial districts, although downtown Columbus remained the focus of retail trade and business activity. During the prosperity of the 1920s, most new growth was in established suburban areas, but Columbus also continued to grow by annexing unincorporated land at the city's edge. The population in 1920 was 237,000, and by 1930 the population of Franklin County was 361,000, with most of those citizens living in Columbus.

It was in this era that downtown Columbus began to emerge in the form that we know today. A devastating flood in 1913 put much of the West Side of the city under water. In the wake of the flood, a program of river control and bridge construction sparked the construction of a civic center for Columbus. A new city hall and police station were complemented by the privately constructed American Insurance Union Citadel, known today as the LeVeque Tower. A State Office Building and Federal District Court building followed in the 1930s.

The Depression slowed business development and population growth—between 1930 and 1940 the county's population grew by only 27,000, But with the start of World War II, Columbus and central Ohio, like much of the country, boomed with war work, hosting such major facilities as the Curtiss-Wright aircraft plant at Port Columbus Airport, and the nearby government supply depot.

In the postwar years Columbus would see some of its most rapid growth. Nearly all of it was in the new suburban areas that blossomed as farmland near the city was converted to housing and commercial strips. Because Columbus was not hemmed in by other municipalities—a condition that would prove a major problem for cities such as Cleveland and Cincinnati—it was able to pursue an aggressive annexation policy that kept the urban boundaries pushing ever outward. The process was greatly aided by freeway development. The Innerbelt around the downtown area came first, followed by the Outerbelt and the Interstate routes. These roads made it feasible to live fairly far from the city's center while still working there; indeed, downtown Columbus even today retains the greatest concentration of jobs in Franklin County.

With the freeways and the suburbs came shopping centers and a whole new series of urban and metropolitan parks, as well as new commercial office complexes and education centers. Some of these new developments were architecturally and economically innovative.

By 1960, the county's population was 683,000, most of it still in Columbus. Suburban growth, however, came at a cost. Urban neighborhoods were gashed by freeways. Jobs and businesses moved out to remote areas and investment in the city core dwindled, though not as severely as in some other places. Columbus suffered all the urban ills typical of American cities in the decades from the 1960s through the 1980s.

Completion of the freeway system in the early 1970s further encouraged development of the suburban fringes. But at the same time a hardy band of urban pioneers began to discover the benefits of urban living. Areas such as German Village, Victorian Village, and Italian Village, where people found well-built homes at bargain prices, soon became the focus of revitalization efforts, even as the departure of retail and demolition of buildings for parking and "urban renewal" projects resulted in a downtown area of as much as 50 percent vacant land.

Since the late 1980s, however, renewed focus on downtown Columbus for office, retail, entertainment, and, in recent years, residential projects has meant a true rebirth of the central city. Condominium and apartment projects have added numerous living units, and thriving nearby areas such as the Short North and the Brewery District have added residential, restaurant, and entertainment space, encouraging a whole new generation of people to live in and near the heart of town.

During the 1990s and into the new century, this downtown rebirth accelerated, spurred by such major projects as the Statehouse restoration; the incorporation of Central High School into the new Center of Science and Industry (COSI); and renovation and expansion of the convention center. Completion of the Nationwide Arena, home of the city's own Blue Jackets hockey team, has triggered many acres of new commercial and residential development in the Arena District, with positive spillover into the adjacent North Market neighborhood. As traditional downtown office buildings have seen tenants leave for new space in the Arena District and elsewhere, these buildings have become available for creatively designed loft-conversion apartments and condominiums.

Residential development in the Brewery District has continued and even accelerated. This neighborhood, as well as German Village and others, has suffered for many decades from being separated by the I-70/I-71 Innerbelt freeway from the downtown core. Planning for freeway improvements now is taking a serious look at caps that can carry streets over the roadway and provide new urban land for development. The successful I-670 Short North Cap, which relinked the convention center and the North Market district with the Short North neighborhood, provides a nationally important model for this effort.

Internationally known architects have left their mark on Columbus in projects such as COSI and the Wexner Center for the Arts on the Ohio State University campus. OSU's new Knowlton School of Architecture has received major attention in architecture and design circles. A huge amount of ongoing construction on the OSU campus is helping the institution hold its place as one of the nation's most important public universities.

Despite the loss of some important historical structures over the years, Columbus still offers a rich variety of historical and contemporary architecture. Some of the best of it can be seen in the pages that follow.

Jeffrey T. Darbee and Edward T. Lentz

AREAS COVERED IN THIS GUIDE

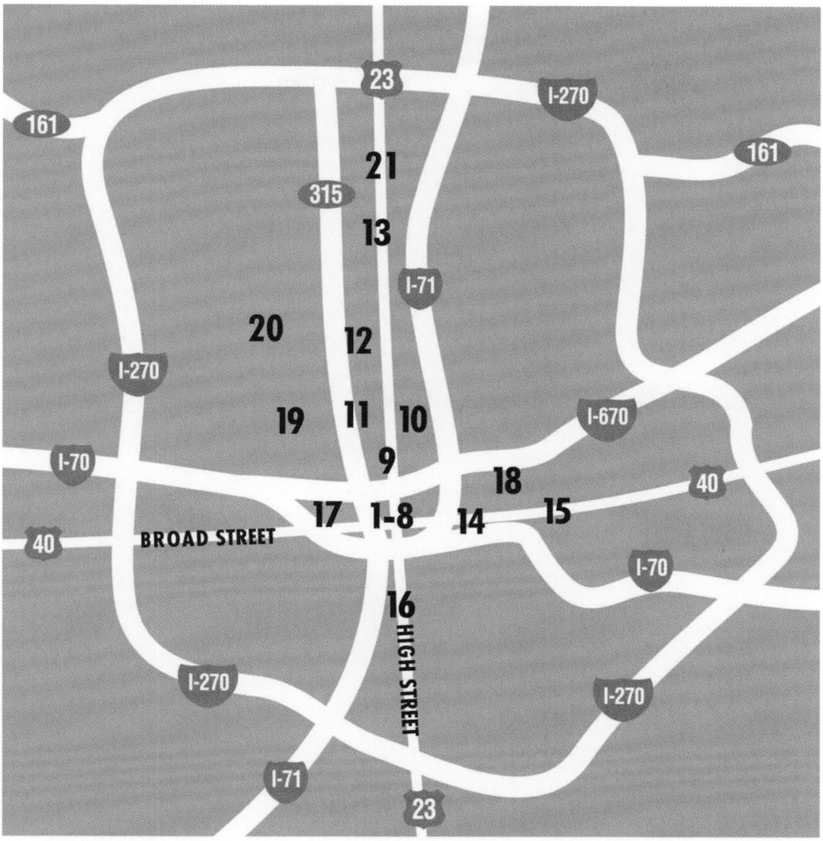

1 CAPITOL SQUARE AREA
2 CIVIC CENTER
3 DOWNTOWN SOUTH HIGH STREET
4 DOWNTOWN EAST SIDE
5 DOWNTOWN EAST BROAD STREET
6 DOWNTOWN NORTH HIGH STREET
7 DOWNTOWN NORTH INNERBELT
8 NORTH MARKET HISTORIC DISTRICT
9 SHORT NORTH HISTORIC DISTRICT
10 ITALIAN VILLAGE HISTORIC DISTRICT
11 VICTORIAN VILLAGE / HARRISON WEST / DENNISON PLACE
12 THE OHIO STATE UNIVERSITY
13 CLINTONVILLE
14 NEAR EAST SIDE
15 BEXLEY
16 GERMAN VILLAGE HISTORIC DISTRICT
17 FRANKLINTON
18 MOUNT VERNON AREA
19 GRANDVIEW HEIGHTS & MARBLE CLIFF
20 UPPER ARLINGTON
21 WORTHINGTON

1 CAPITOL SQUARE AREA
2 CIVIC CENTER
3 DOWNTOWN SOUTH HIGH STREET
4 DOWNTOWN EAST SIDE
5 DOWNTOWN EAST BROAD STREET
6 DOWNTOWN NORTH HIGH STREET
7 DOWNTOWN NORTH INNERBELT
8 NORTH MARKET HISTORIC DISTRICT

Downtown

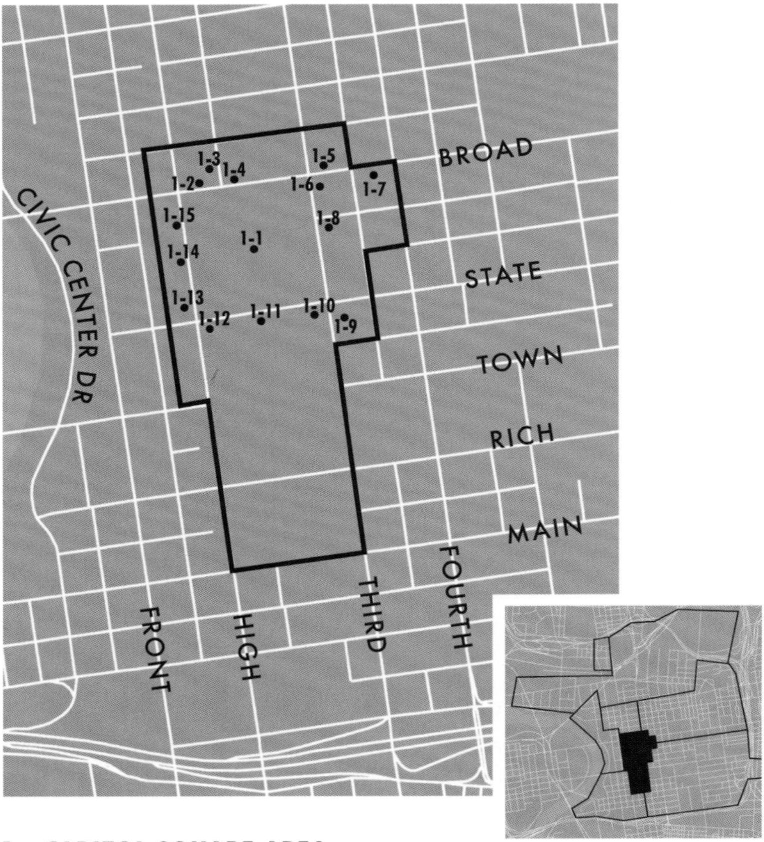

1 CAPITOL SQUARE AREA

1

Capitol Square Area

Capitol Square

Although other buildings on the square may be newer, larger, and much taller, the Capitol's historic stature overshadows them all. More than forty administrations—beginning with Governor Salmon P. Chase's in 1856—have directed state government from this building. Throughout its history, presidents, politicians, and protesters have used the Statehouse as a rallying place.

Capitol Square's magnetic presence draws thousands of visitors each year. The Ohio Statehouse, a National Historic Landmark, is widely considered by experts to be one of the country's finest examples of Greek Revival architecture. The square, with its landscaped grounds and monumental sculptural elements, is an inviting place for people to relax and enjoy a rich environment steeped in Ohio history.

1-1a

1-1b

1-1c

1-1

NHL, NR, CR

OHIO STATEHOUSE

Southeast corner of Broad and High streets, bounded by Broad, Third, State, and High streets

1839–61

Architects: Henry Ustick Walter, Cincinnati; Alexander J. Davis, New York City; William Russell West, Cincinnati; Nathan B. Kelly, Columbus; Isaiah Rogers, Cincinnati

Greek Revival

SENATE BUILDING (STATEHOUSE ANNEX)

1901

Architect: Samuel Hannaford & Sons, Cincinnati

Neoclassical Revival

CAPITOL ATRIUM

1996

Architects: Schooley Caldwell Associates; Moody•Nolan Ltd., Inc., Columbus

AIAO, AIAC, CLF

RENOVATION AND ADDITION

1989–96

Architects: Schooley Caldwell Associates, Columbus; Moody•Nolan Ltd., Inc., Columbus

The restrained Greek Revival grandeur of Ohio's statehouse belies its turbulent past. In 1812, over the objections of former state capitals Chillicothe and Zanesville, Ohio's General Assembly chose Columbus as the permanent state capital. Four investors from Franklinton proposed creating a capital city near Wolf's Ridge, on the east bank of the Scioto, and offered to donate ten acres for state buildings. In return, they received construction contracts for a statehouse, a state office building, and other structures. After platting out a public square with the Capitol on the southwest corner, they sold the surrounding lots of wooded wilderness for $50,000.

By the 1830s the original buildings were too small for a rapidly developing state. In 1838 the General Assembly created a three-member commission to oversee construction of a new statehouse. The commission advertised a design competition in several large eastern cities, as well as throughout Ohio. Sixty submissions were received and three were selected for prizes.

Statehouse construction began in 1839, with much of the work being undertaken by convict laborers from the nearby Ohio Penitentiary. The construction took twenty-two years and withstood several bureaucratic delays. In 1840 lawmakers repealed the statehouse construction law, and building stopped for four years. Even after the old capitol burned in 1852, controversy continued to delay construction of a new one. Legislators not only changed architects, but also worked on the designs themselves. Cost overruns, a cholera epidemic, and political discord caused further delay, and the building was not completed until 1861. Despite all these difficulties, a cohesive final design emerged. Its severe simplicity and bold, distinctive form give the Statehouse its arresting visual power.

As required by the competition program, all three winning designs were Greek Revival in style and featured porticoes, square pilasters separating window bays, exterior vertical bays, and a central cupola with an interior dome. The finished Statehouse is remarkably true to the original conception.

Before entering the Capitol, look for fossils in the building's locally quarried limestone walls. Once in the rotunda, notice the floor, composed of nearly 5,000 pieces of American, Italian, and Portuguese marble, and be sure to look up at the state seal high above.

In the 1990s the Statehouse complex underwent a $116 million renovation and restoration, including construction of a new Capitol Atrium. This addition, placed between the original Capitol and the annex, features locally quarried limestone, elegant skylights that connect the addition to the adjacent buildings, and specifically commissioned light fixtures. A large marble map of Ohio is a popular feature in the lower-level Visitor's Center.

Inside the Statehouse, workers have removed alterations made during the building's 140-year life. For instance, the Capitol originally had 53 rooms, all of which had natural lighting; when the renovation began, it had 317 rooms! The original 53 have now been restored.

The Senate Building was originally constructed in 1901 to house the Ohio Judiciary, most notably the Supreme Court of Ohio. Also built of local limestone, it was designed to be sympathetic to, but not imitate, the Statehouse. Observe how its Neoclassical design balances well with the older building, yet lets the Senate Building make its own architectural statement. The pilasters separating the window bays, for example, echo those at the Capitol. The building has been completely renovated and retains its turn-of-the-century character and detailing. Look for the ornate stair hall/rotunda, a principal feature of the original building that has been carefully preserved.

The Ohio Veterans Plaza is located on Third Street, immediately adjacent to the Senate Building. Its eighty-eight flags representing the state's counties (installed for special events and holidays), stone walls inscribed with excerpts from veterans' letters, and a pair of fountains create a dignified space for remembrance and quiet contemplation.

1-2

CAPITOL TRUST BUILDING

8 East Broad Street
Circa 1906
Architect: Frank L. Packard, Columbus
Early-Twentieth-Century Skyscraper

SIXTEEN EAST BROAD BUILDING (HAYDEN BUILDING)

16 East Broad Street
Circa 1900
Architect: Frank L. Packard, Columbus
Early-Twentieth-Century Skyscraper

HAYDEN BUILDING (HAYDEN-CLINTON BANK BUILDING)

20 East Broad Street
1869

RENOVATION
1920
High Victorian Italianate

This cluster of buildings at Broad and High reflects a period of dramatic change in building form, structure, and architectural detailing; looking at them, you can see how office buildings evolved from the late nineteenth to the early twentieth centuries.

The bank building at 20 East Broad is the oldest, built by Peter Hayden, a local coal, brick, iron, and railroad magnate. This brick building has bearing walls that support the floors and roof. Its sandstone front is executed in a restrained High Victorian Italianate style. Note that its windows have both round and segmental arches. The quoins at the corners of the building contrast with the walls and projecting central bay. The heavy cornice above completes the composition. The rusticated terra-cotta storefront on the ground floor dates from the 1920s alteration, as do the bay windows on the east side. As the plaque on the building's southeast corner attests, Trinity Episcopal Church, built in 1834, originally occupied this site.

In contrast, the two buildings to the west are true skyscrapers. Rather than masonry bearing walls, they have steel frames to support the floors and roofs, and because of their steel frames, they have much more window space than

1-2

the Hayden-Clinton Bank Building. In the early years of this century, each skyscraper had a definite bottom, middle, and top, corresponding to the base, shaft, and capital of a classical column. Looking at the Capitol Trust and the Sixteen East Broad buildings, you can still easily identify the three parts.

The Capital Trust Building once had a three-story base. The first floor had an entrance door on the left with two rectangular windows. Three arched windows with keystones were on the second floor, and three square windows were on the third floor. This part of the facade was most likely terra-cotta, similar to that at the top of the building. Although the 16 East Broad Building has also had extensive alterations to its street level and its windows, it retains original details. Look for the circled H's in the terra-cotta for the owner, Peter Hayden.

Lynn Street–Pearl Alley

The Lynn Street–Pearl Alley area contains several interesting older buildings. More than twenty years ago, the city cleaned up and paved these intersecting alleys to make the area more appealing. Several restaurants are now located here. On Lynn Street, look for two small structures: the side-by-side Wheeler and Braun buildings, which date from about 1915. The Wheeler Building at 52 Lynn Street shows Renaissance Revival influences, like the large arch around the central windows on the second and third floors. The Braun Building, at 66 Lynn Street, has three clusters of three windows set into its brick facade. Around the corner, on Pearl Alley, is the Ringside Café.

1-3

1-3

RINGSIDE CAFÉ

19 North Pearl Alley
Circa 1910
Architects: Howell & Thomas, Columbus

Don't overlook one of the smallest and most interesting buildings in downtown Columbus. The Ringside Café, sitting in the shadow of the Rhodes State Office Tower, is one of a few surviving old-time Columbus haunts. Built on the site of a burned-out saloon, it was originally known as the Chamber of Commerce Café when the Chamber was located in the Board of Trade Building, then on the site now occupied by the Rhodes Office Tower. When the Chamber objected to the café's use of its name, the owner covered the name with carved grapes and vines, which you can still see over the door. After Prohibition, the next owner chose the name "Ringside Café" because prizefights were held in the Board of Trade auditorium.

The one-story brick structure with its limestone foundation looks unassuming, but the warm and appealing interior is intimate in scale, reminiscent of an English pub. The Ringside has always been a favorite of newspaper people and politicians.

1-4
AIAO, AIAC

RHODES STATE OFFICE TOWER

30 East Broad Street

1974

Architects: Brubaker/Brandt, Columbus; Dalton•Dalton•Little•Newport, Cleveland

As the city's tallest skyscraper, Rhodes State Office Tower is a distinctive, commanding presence on Capitol Square. This forty-one-story building's form and massing are complex. The exterior is of dark gray glass and red flame granite. Gazing around Capitol Square, you can see this same reddish-pink Italian granite on the Huntington Building, its color reflected again in the color of the Wyandotte Building. The architects carried this rich stone surface through to the tower's three-story lobby. While you walk around the square, if you glance back at this building occasionally you will notice some subtle changes each time you do, because of the tower's series of intersecting rectangular planes.

The asymmetrical base reflects the scale of the earlier buildings adjacent to the Rhodes Tower. The entrance is set back from the plane of the southwest corner of the building, thus creating a small plaza area. A bronze sculpture of the building's namesake, four-term Ohio Governor James A. Rhodes, is located in the plaza facing Capitol Square.

1-5

CHASE BANK (BANK ONE, COLUMBUS CENTER)

100 East Broad Street

1965

Architects: Harrison & Abramovitz, New York; Granzow, Guss & Harder, Columbus

Built as the City National Bank Building just off Capitol Square, this structure brought the 1960s vision of a contemporary office building to Columbus: it is bold, boxy, and tall, with no extraneous ornamentation; its strong vertical lines rise unbroken from ground to roof. The twenty-four-floor building is set back from East Broad Street, forming a plaza several steps below street level, the first plaza of its kind in downtown Columbus.

Chase Bank's extra-tall ground floor houses a banking lobby. A separate entry lobby for upper-floor offices is in the low extension of the building's northwest corner.

Note that each elevation of the building is a geometric interplay of tinted glass and metallic elements. Strong projecting pilasters run from the ground to the parapet. Accenting the building's height, the pilasters divide each side of the building into five distinct bays, or sections. Within each bay, mullions, similar to narrow pilasters, divide the windows and the spandrels below them into five parts. The dark-colored spandrels recede visually, making the main vertical pilasters even more apparent. Each elevation terminates in the simple horizontal line of the parapet.

1-6

1-6

NR, CR

TRINITY EPISCOPAL CHURCH

125 East Broad Street

1869

Architect: Gordon W. Lloyd, Detroit

Gothic Revival

PARISH HOUSE

1910

Architects: Howell & Thomas, Columbus

PARISH HOUSE ADDITION

1976

Architects: Nitschke, Godwin, Böhm, Columbus

EXTERIOR RENOVATION

1994

Architects: Schooley Caldwell Associates, Columbus

INTERIOR RENOVATION

2006

Architects: Rogers Krajnak, Columbus

Founded in 1817, the Episcopal parish that built this church met in various places, including its own 1834 church farther west, at 20 East Broad Street, where the Hayden-Clinton Bank now stands. Construction of the current church took three years under the guidance of Gordon W. Lloyd, a transplanted Englishman trained in Gothic Revival architecture.

Trinity Episcopal's weathered sandstone exterior and fanciful Gothic design contrast dramatically with the other buildings on Capitol Square. The church's main west exterior is asymmetrical, with a square buttressed tower at the northwest corner. Several elements, like its numerous buttresses, rock-faced ashlar walls, crockets, crenellated parapets, and pointed arch openings, accent the church's Gothic character. Inside, the outstanding features are the hammerbeam roof framing in the nave and the carved altar screen dating from 1912.

In 1910 the congregation added crenellations to the tower and constructed a parish house on the east side of the church. The architects used similar materials on the Parish House to complement the design and features of the church. The extra story added to the Parish House in 1976 is clad in dark-colored metal to blend in with the stone walls.

1-7

1-8

Dispatch
OHIO'S
GREATEST
HOME NEWSPAPER
119 YEARS OF SERVICE
THE DISPATCH

1-7

NATIONAL CITY BANK PLAZA (OHIO NATIONAL PLAZA)

155 East Broad Street

1976

Architects: Skidmore, Owings & Merrill, Chicago; Dan A. Carmichael, Columbus

The National City Bank building is a cluster of square towers set on an L-shaped site. This bundled-tube configuration is similar to that of Chicago's Sears Tower. Faced in a cream-colored travertine marble, the clustered towers have individual windows rather than horizontal or vertical bands of windows. They are vertically proportioned and glazed with a dark-tinted glass. Note the rigid grid pattern of nine windows per floor on each tower. The tallest tower has twenty-four floors.

The building rises from a three-story glass structure containing the main banking lobby along Broad Street and commercial and office space along Third Street. This structure is dark glass, which provides contrast to the light-colored tower. Observe how it wraps respectfully around Trinity Episcopal Church: the color, scale, height, and setback actually accent the historic church and create a pedestrian scale along Broad and Third streets.

1-8

COLUMBUS DISPATCH BUILDING

34 South Third Street

1925

Architects: Harvey H. Heistand, Columbus; Snyder Babbitt & Mathews, Columbus

Second Renaissance Revival elements

An attractive addition to the square, the Columbus Dispatch Building has been altered very little since 1925. The building shows strong influence of the Second Renaissance Revival style, apparent in the use of rusticated stonework, the relatively plain upper floors, and the strong projecting decorative cornice on the upper part of the facade

These features appear only on the front part of this five-story building, which measures three bays by two. Originally, the building was only four stories high and the rear was brick with seven bays. The fifth floor was added later, as was a brick addition (now removed) which once extended to Fourth Street.

The large neon sign that sits atop the building has become a visual landmark on Capitol Square. It features the *Dispatch*'s claim to be "Ohio's Greatest Home Newspaper."

1-9

1-9
NR, CR

BRICKER & ECKLER BUILDING (OLD, OLD POST OFFICE, U.S. POST OFFICE AND COURTHOUSE)

100 South Third Street
1887
Architect: John T. Harris, Columbus
Romanesque Revival

ADDITION
1907–12
Architect: James Knox Taylor, Washington, DC
High Victorian Gothic

CLF

RENOVATION
1986
Architects: Böhm-NBBJ, Columbus

Originally constructed as the city's main post office, the original portion of this building was only about one-third the size of the current building. The enlargement and remodeling in the early twentieth century were so thorough that they resulted in a single unified style.

The original building was Romanesque Revival in style and featured round-arched window openings topped by heavy hoodmolds, projecting stone bands between floors, and three slate-covered hipped roofs. The walls were tan rock-faced Berea sandstone, with smooth sandstone used for trim.

Beginning in 1907, the Post Office more than doubled in size. The addition, for which builders used the same sandstone, was placed to the south of the original building on the corner of State and Third streets. The addition and the alterations are in the High Victorian Gothic style. Among the elements of this style are pointed arch openings, buttresses (or pillars added for support), and Gothic-inspired ornamentation. The entire composition is unified by the warm red tile roof, which replaced the original slate roof.

During the building's rehabilitation for use as law offices in 1986, the architects retained a number of significant features, including the carved oak postal screen wall on the main floor, the elegant marble staircase, carved oak wainscoting, and wood-coffered ceilings. The courtroom was also retained and now serves as a boardroom.

1-10a

1-10b

1-10
AIAC

HYATT ON CAPITOL SQUARE

75 East State Street
1984
Architects: Patrick + Associates, Columbus

CAPITOL SQUARE OFFICE BUILDING

65 East State Street
1984
Architects: Abramovitz, Harris & Kingsland, New York City

The hotel and the office building next to it form a pair of triangular towers nearly touching at one corner. Although both have horizontal banded windows, notice the larger floor-to-floor dimensions in the office building. Both exteriors are extremely simple and unadorned.

The primary entrances to both buildings sit well back from the street to create a quiet plaza. The plaza's central feature is a monumental bronze sculpture, *Naiads,* by artist Jack Greaves. While striking even during the winter months, the sculpture becomes the centerpiece of a fountain during warm weather, when the shaded plaza is transformed into a popular downtown gathering spot.

South of the plaza is the entry to a shop-lined interior passage leading to Columbus City Center. The lobbies of both the hotel and the office building also open onto this passage, providing all-weather pedestrian access to City Center.

1-11a

1-11b

DOWNTOWN

1-11

NHL, NR, CLF

OHIO THEATRE (LOEW'S OHIO THEATRE)

39 East State Street

1928

Architect: Thomas W. Lamb, New York City

Beaux-Arts exterior, Movie Palace interior

JOHN AND DOROTHY GALBREATH PAVILION

55 East State Street

1984

Architects: Hardy Holzman Pfeiffer, New York City; Philip Markwood Architects, Columbus

The Ohio Theatre, now a National Historic Landmark, came perilously close to demolition before being rescued by the Columbus Association for the Performing Arts (CAPA) in 1969. CAPA has owned and operated this theater since, while conducting a careful, ongoing restoration.

The Ohio Theatre was part of the Loew's chain, the creation of Marcus Loew, who later helped form the film production company Metro-Goldwyn-Mayer. For his Columbus movie palace Loew chose theater designer Thomas W. Lamb, who displayed his versatility by simultaneously designing the much more restrained and quite different Palace Theatre on West Broad Street.

The Ohio Theatre's severe stone and terra-cotta Beaux-Arts exterior belies its sumptuous interior finishes. It is difficult to believe that it took only about a year to build. Look closely at the ornate ticket booth at the sidewalk; it hints that something special awaits beyond the brass doors. Best described as Moorish Baroque in character, the interior contains a small multistory entry lobby of gracious proportions. Other interior features include large pieces of black glass, a gorgeous stained-glass ceiling, and a two-and-one-half-ton chandelier. For a glimpse of the original theater, see the photographs on the mezzanine.

Because the original lobby was too small for the building's new use as a concert and live performance venue, the Galbreath Pavilion was constructed to the east to provide additional space for intermissions and special events, rehearsal space, dressing rooms, and administrative offices. Note that the maroon glazed terra-cotta on the west wall mimics a stage curtain. The State Street side of this compatible contemporary addition is buff brick to reflect the original theater's character. Along its east side are theater and office entrances. A glass-roofed walkway leads to Columbus City Center.

The Ohio Theatre is well worth a visit for one of the many theatrical and musical events held here; the auditorium seats nearly 2,900 and the acoustics are excellent.

1-12

1-12
Fifth Third Center (Beggs Building)

BEGGS BUILDING

21 East State Street
1928
Architects: Miller & Reeves, Columbus
Art Moderne

RENOVATION
1991
Architects: Acock Schlegel, Columbus

FIFTH THIRD CENTER

1998
Architects: Acock Associates, Columbus

The Beggs Building has been a landmark on Capitol Square for over seven decades. Working in the Art Moderne style, the architects used terra-cotta, giving the exterior a three-dimensional decorative quality. Note the stylized flora, fauna, and geometric designs typical of the period.

The eight projecting pilasters are the strongest element of the design, enhanced by the intermediate pilasters between the windows and the decorative horizontal spandrels. The cornice (since removed) was especially ornate, with stylized figureheads and a castellated parapet. The Art Moderne style is not the building's only echo of the past; it also uses the distinct base, shaft, and capital composition typical of the earlier Commercial style.

The original twelve-story building has been considerably altered. In the 1950s Wendell Beggs, son of the developer, added a penthouse, where he lived until the mid-1960s. In 1991 the penthouse was removed as part of a multimillion-dollar remodeling that extensively altered the interior. As well as adding two floors, the architects opened up new interior space by relocating the mechanical and electrical systems, restrooms, and stairs to a vertical spine on the back of the building.

In 1998 a twenty-three-story companion building was added on the corner of State and High streets, connecting to the original Beggs Building. According to *Business First,* it was the first commercial high-rise in Columbus in a decade. Though it does not repeat the elements of the original building, it does complement it with its color, materials, and restrained design.

1-13

1-13
AIAC

VERN RIFFE CENTER FOR GOVERNMENT AND THE ARTS

77 South High Street
1989
Architects: Böhm-NBBJ, Columbus
Postmodern

Named for the long-time Speaker of the Ohio House of Representatives, the Vern Riffe Center reflects and complements the Ohio Judicial Center (formerly the Ohio Departments of State Building) across Front Street. Note the Riffe Center's smooth white stone exterior and green metal roof, replicating the most notable features of the older building. Observe also how the center's rather small window bands and the pilastered columns on the upper floors are reminiscent of the Ohio Judicial Center.

In its thirty-three floors, Riffe Center houses the offices of the governor, lieutenant governor, members of the House of Representatives, and numerous departments of state government. The Center also contains three theaters and a daycare center. In the state art gallery on the first floor, note the herringbone-design wood floor. Tunnels connect the Riffe Center to Huntington Center as well as to the Statehouse.

1-14

1-14

HUNTINGTON CENTER

41 South High Street
1984
Architects: Skidmore, Owings & Merrill, Chicago

The thirty-seven-story Huntington Center has a commanding presence and distinctive profile on Capitol Square. Its formal and symmetrical design respect the Ohio Statehouse directly across the street. The H-shaped, notch-back arrangement of this building's principal east and west facades makes it distinctive in the city, giving it a character that constantly changes according to angle of view and light conditions. This is another building you will want to look back to from time to time as you move around Capitol Square.

Notice how the massive exterior trusses define a series of multistory interior atriums and express one aspect of the building's structure. The innovative H-shape not only makes for an interesting facade, but also creates multiple corner offices on every floor. The building is also distinctive for its use of tinted glass and red granite with a flame finish.

The lower level and ground floor of the Huntington Center house retail stores and offices, while the mezzanine provides access to a downtown hotel and a private club. Tunnels connect the center to various state government buildings.

1-15

1-15

HUNTINGTON NATIONAL BANK BUILDING

17 South High Street
Circa 1900; 1926
Architects: Snyder & Babbitt, Columbus
Second Renaissance Revival

In 1916 Huntington Bank, a local institution dating from 1866, established its offices on Capitol Square. Its first home was the twelve-story Harrison Building, one of the tallest on the square when it was built in 1900. However, by the mid-1920s the Harrison was much too small for the fast-growing banking firm. In 1925 the bank began adding a new structure against the north wall of the Harrison Building. On the east side a new fine-grained limestone facade in the Second Renaissance Revival style blended the two buildings. Note the heavily rusticated surface of the lower floors and corners, large central entrance, multiple belt course, and decorative cornice typical of this style.

During construction of the Huntington Center next door, the architect designed the bank building's brick west wall with stucco, giving it a contemporary look reminiscent of the rustication on the east facade. To see one of the Harrison Building's original brick walls, look on the building's south wall, one bay back from the east (or front) facade.

During business hours, visit the impressive 1927 Tiffany banking lobby, which occupies nearly all of the ground floor. Its highly decorated flat ceiling, banking counter, tellers' cages, and decorative elevator doors create the feeling of a prosperous 1920s financial institution.

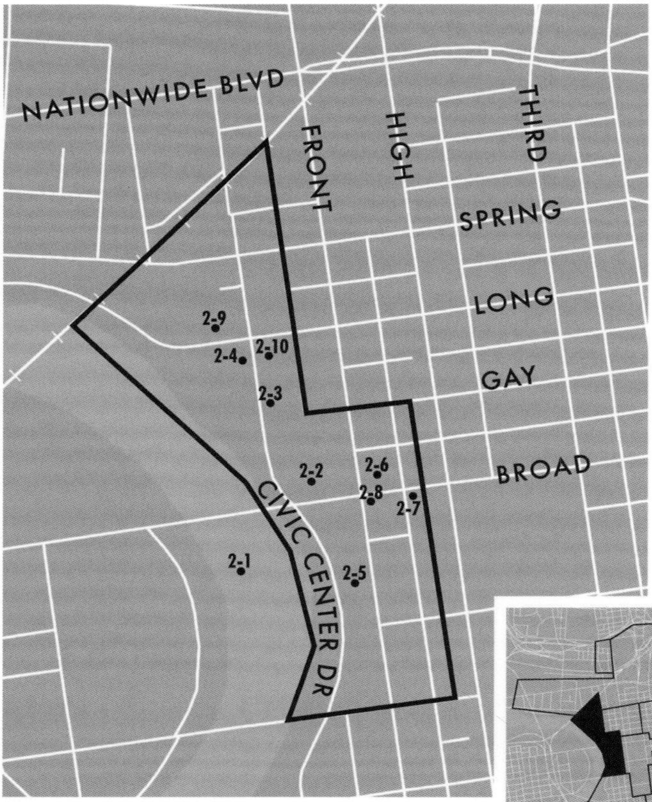

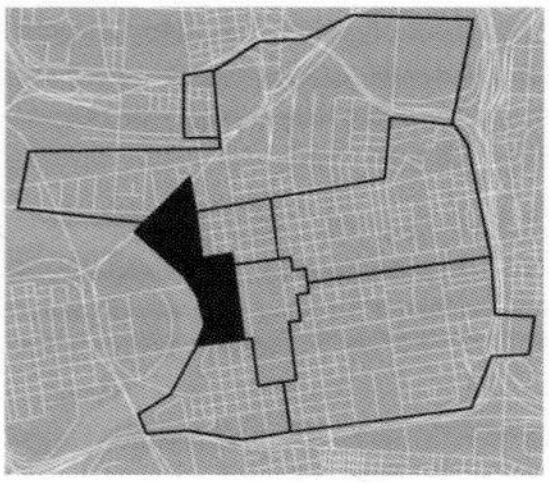

2 CIVIC CENTER

2

Civic Center

Little by little, the Scioto River has shaped Columbus's destiny. If not for the river's frequent flooding, Ohio's early lawmakers might well have chosen Franklinton, the first settlement in the area, as the site of the state capital. Throughout the nineteenth century, floods were a fact of life in Franklinton and other low-lying parts of Columbus. Then, in March 1913, the river's raging floodwaters washed away four bridges and left 20,000 people homeless.

This tragedy provided the impetus for civic leaders to take action to minimize the dangers of future flooding while at the same time making public improvements that eventually led to the creation of the Civic Center. Buildings on both sides of the Scioto River were cleared, the river was increased to nearly twice its original width, and a concrete retaining wall was built along the east bank. Three new bridges were constructed in the Neoclassical style, and between 1924 and 1934 public buildings were constructed along both the east and west banks, creating a unified and cohesive Civic Center.

2-1

CR

Scioto River Bridges Parks and Civic Center Drive

TOWN STREET BRIDGE

1917

MAIN STREET BRIDGE (recently demolished)

1935

Designer: Paul Maeter, Columbus

BROAD STREET BRIDGE

1992

Architects: Burgess & Niple, Columbus

BICENTENNIAL PARK

1976

Landscape Architect: Roger Wells, Parks Superintendent

BATTELLE RIVERFRONT PARK

Landscape Architects: Böhm NBBJ

Even though the Civic Center plan eventually developed a series of striking new buildings, the heart of the project is Civic Center Drive, its floodwall, and the Scioto River bridges at Broad, Town, and Main streets. Executed in a design employing classical elements, these riverfront improvements provide an elegant setting for the buildings making up the Civic Center.

Observe the floodwalls, for example. Flat panels are separated by rusticated pilasters, while at the sidewalk level a heavy concrete balustrade extends the entire length of the floodwall.

The current Broad Street Bridge is a worthy successor to the original, which dated from the early twentieth century. Though it has only five spans instead of the original's seven, resulting in shallower arches without the semicircular shape typical of the classically inspired overall Civic Center design, the new bridge is rich in materials and detail. It includes desirable features not found on the original, like the rounded lookouts along the sidewalk and access stairs leading down to the river itself.

The Civic Center is lined with parks that enhance the public spaces along the riverfront. Bicentennial Park, located at the south end of the Civic Center, was

2-1

completed in 1976. Its major feature is a large fountain, which sprays water high in the air. Battelle Park, located across from City Hall, features a walkway that extends down to the level of the river. The newest Civic Center park is North Bank Park, across from the Arena District (and the former site of the Ohio Penitentiary). Its central feature is a glass-and-brick building located at the foot of Neil Avenue. Terraces provide a spectacular view of the downtown skyline and the Columbus Civic Center. See the separate entry for nearby North Bank Park. The Main Street and Town Street bridges are slated for replacement.

2-2

2-2

COLUMBUS CITY HALL

90 West Broad Street
1928; 1936; 1949
Architects: Allied Architects Association of Columbus
Neoclassical Revival

City Hall occupies a prominent site on the Scioto River's sloping east bank. Note the large statue of Christopher Columbus in the plaza facing Broad Street. The Marconi Boulevard elevation most strongly evokes the classical architecture on which the building's design was based. Notice how the portico with eight large Ionic columns and a full entablature give the building a monumental presence on the river. The other three sides have pilasters rather than freestanding columns. Originally the building was U-shaped, with an open courtyard and garden in the center. In 1936 an east wing was added, and the central courtyard was enclosed in 1949.

City Hall's smooth Indiana limestone contrasts with the finely detailed polished brown marble entrance surrounds. During the week, stop in to see the City Council Chamber on the second floor. Restored in 1986, the chamber combines classical and Art Deco design elements. Also note the interior details, such as the use of marble (especially the ornate spiral staircase outside the City Council Chamber) and the numerous brass decorative details.

2-3

OLD CENTRAL POLICE STATION

120 West Gay Street
1928
Architects: Allied Architects Association of Columbus
Second Renaissance Revival

The design of the old Central Police Station, built as part of the Civic Center, is compatible with both City Hall to the south and the Joseph P. Kinneary United States Courthouse to the west. The building is clad in fine-grained limestone with gray granite entrance steps.

The L-shaped building shows Second Renaissance Revival style influences. Look for these elements: the rusticated first floor facade, a modestly projecting cornice above the fifth floor, and the plain, unadorned floors in between. The windows are steel casement sash; those on the second and third floors are separated by metal spandrels. Note that the main entrance is the angled central bay opening to the southwest. Upper-floor windows in this bay are set behind the smooth round columns flanked by square pilasters.

2-4

2-4

JOSEPH P. KINNEARY UNITED STATES COURTHOUSE (U.S. POST OFFICE AND COURTHOUSE, OLD POST OFFICE)

83 Marconi Boulevard
1934
Architects: Richards, McCarty & Bulford, Columbus
Neoclassical Revival

RENOVATION
1996
Architects: Schooley Caldwell Associates, Columbus

The Old Post Office's wide pilasters with deeply recessed windows between them give the building a strong, stately presence. The sandstone and marble facade gives the building a warm, rich tone. The exterior is very plain; its minimal detailing is classically inspired and confined largely to the upper levels above the windows. As you walk along the river to see the west facade, notice how strong belt courses divide the building into three parts. On the north side, a truss-roofed garage and a free-standing colonnade are unusual features.

The northernmost building in the Civic Center group, the Old Post Office replaced the Old, Old Post Office at State and Third streets. The main post office moved to Twin Rivers Drive west of downtown in 1969, but the federal courts and several federal offices are still housed here. The building was renamed for Judge Kinneary in 1998.

2-5
NR, CR

OHIO JUDICIAL CENTER (OHIO DEPARTMENTS OF STATE BUILDING, OHIO STATE OFFICE BUILDING)

65 South Front Street

1933

Architect: Harry Hake, Cincinnati

Art Moderne

AIAO, AIAC, CLF

RENOVATION

2004

Architects: Schooley Caldwell Associates, Columbus; Moody•Nolan Ltd., Columbus; Feinknopf Macioce Schappa, Columbus (exterior)

Only a block off Capitol Square, the Ohio Judicial Center is one of the state's premier examples of the Art Moderne style. Originally built as a state office building and housing a variety of state departments through the years, the building was renovated for use by the judicial branch of Ohio's government.

Across the river from Central High School, this fourteen-story white marble building has a distinctive copper roof. Although the exterior appears austere from a distance, closer inspection reveals ornamentation and inscriptions that celebrate the rich history of the state of Ohio. Particularly noteworthy are the bronze doors along Civic Center Drive and the two large stone carvings on the Front Street elevation. The carvings represent tall, stylized human figures flanked by pairs of animals—rams in the south carving and felines in the north carving.

During its original construction, the architect employed nationally recognized artists to create decorative elements for the building, depicting Ohio history and industry. The public spaces on the ground and first-floor levels of the building include bas-reliefs, painted murals, mosaics, and decorative metals, all of which are fully integrated into the architecture of the building.

The most impressive interior space, the former Hearing Room #2, is now used as a courtroom by the Supreme Court. The room is well scaled and proportioned. The walls are covered with rich paneling and damask fabric. An ornamental ceiling with murals celebrating the five states formed from the old Northwest Territory, and a newly carved bench make this dignified and solemn space ideal for use by the Supreme Court of Ohio. The hearing rooms at the north and south ends of the building also have painted wall murals depicting the development of Ohio.

2-5

A grand concourse extends through the building from north to south, connecting the courtroom and the smaller hearing rooms. The two-story space retains its original marble surfaces and ceiling light fixtures. The elevator lobby features decorative bronze elevator doors symbolizing the four seasons and the four elements of nature. Mosaics adorn the north and south walls of the elevator lobby.

The Civic Center Drive lobby is notable for its Native American theme. It includes bronze bas-reliefs of Ohio's most famous Native American leaders, light fixtures decorated with arrows, and colorful mosaic tile ceilings.

Upper floors house offices and the Supreme Court Law Library. The Library Reading Room, at the north end of the building, is decorated with a series of murals depicting the history of the written word.

2-6

2-6
NR, CR

LEVEQUE TOWER (AMERICAN INSURANCE UNION CITADEL, LINCOLN-LEVEQUE TOWER)

50 West Broad Street
1927
Architect: C. Howard Crane, Detroit
Art Moderne

PALACE THEATRE (KEITH PALACE THEATRE, RKO PALACE)

34 West Broad Street
1926
Architect: Thomas W. Lamb, New York City

A true landmark in Columbus since it opened, LeVeque Tower is still probably the city's best-known skyscraper. At forty-four stories, it was Ohio's tallest and the world's fifth-tallest building at the time of its construction; pilots dubbed it the "first aerial lighthouse." It remained the loftiest building in town until 1974, when the Rhodes State Office Tower was completed. The LeVeque Tower also includes the Palace Theatre, one of downtown's three surviving historic theaters.

The exterior of the tower is clad in white "oak bark" terra-cotta molded into textured blocks resembling cut stone. Ornate terra-cotta sculptures and bas-reliefs give the building a lively facade with considerable detail. Note the eagles atop the wide pilasters flanking the entrances; they have wingspans of twenty feet. From a distance the exterior surface looks flat and smooth, accentuating the height of the tower. Up close, however, the terra-cotta facade's medallions, garlands, and crests become visible and you can see how complex the surface really is.

The office building is composed of a tall tower at the southwest corner flanked by two eighteen-story wings. The Palace Theatre is entered from Broad Street, and its 2,827-seat auditorium fills the northeast quadrant of the building.

The Palace was designed as a vaudeville house and movie theater. Its interior is decorated with classically inspired details. The entrance lobby, sweeping central staircase, and large auditorium establish the character of this grand early-twentieth-century theater. The Columbus Association for the Performing Arts, which also owns the Ohio Theatre, acquired the Palace in 1989.

2-7

2-7
NR

WYANDOTTE BUILDING

21 West Broad Street
1897
Architect: Daniel Hudson Burnham, Chicago
Chicago School Skyscraper Commercial

RENOVATION
1978
Architect: Richard Palencar, Columbus

The eleven-story Wyandotte Building is the city's first skyscraper as well as an example of Chicago School architecture and a wonderful sample of work by one of the true pioneers of American architecture, Daniel Hudson Burnham. Like many early skyscrapers, the building is constructed of a masonry skin over a steel frame. The vertical rows of bay windows, which are a prominent visual feature, were one of Burnham's trademarks, designed to provide light, ventilation, and extra floor space on crowded city blocks. Also note the elegantly simple, restrained ornamentation.

The Wyandotte Building also has a typical Commercial Style design; note how its street facade is similar to the three elements of a classical column. The lower two floors, comprising the building's base, have battered walls, which impart a sense of stability and permanence. The nine-story shaft is topped off by a very simple cornice. Note also the detailed terra-cotta ornaments, particularly around the entrance, which contrast with the simplicity of the brickwork on the upper floors.

The Wyandotte Building originally housed the Wyandotte Building & Loan Company and other commercial tenants. In 1916 the State of Ohio purchased the skyscraper for state offices, and in 1975 local investors purchased the Wyandotte and rehabilitated the interior for commercial office use.

The Columbus Chapter of the American Institute of Architects is located in this building.

2-8

DOWNTOWN

2-8

HUNTINGTON PLAZA

37 West Broad Street

1965

Architects: Skidmore Owings & Merrill, Chicago; Benham, Richards & Armstrong, Columbus

Built on the site of a theater and other commercial structures, the Huntington Mortgage Building is one of the earliest of the contemporary downtown buildings on and near Capitol Square. The Huntington National Bank had been a presence on the Columbus business scene since 1866, and the West Broad Street building was built for its mortgage subsidiary and other tenants.

Broad Street slopes down toward the Scioto River in this area, so the Huntington Mortgage Building was built on a plaza that gave it a level site. This placed the plaza at street level on the east, but a full floor above the street on the west along Front Street. The plaza is a pleasant, shady park.

The building hovers above its glass lobby, which is recessed behind rows of structural columns; the mass of the building is cantilevered out beyond the column line. The sturdy concrete grid of the four facades reflects the rhythms and patterns of traditional skyscraper design—note this kinship by comparison to the 1897 Wyandotte Building just to the east.

2-9

AMERICAN ELECTRIC POWER COMPANY BUILDING

1 Riverside Plaza

1983

Architects: Abramovitz Harris & Kingsland, New York City

During the 1970s and 1980s, several major firms in New York City, including American Electric Power Company (AEP), relocated their corporate headquarters to Columbus. Clad in a light stone, AEP's thirty-one-story headquarters is a multi-sided structure oriented principally to the east and south. Its windows form horizontal bands set deeply into the building's stone surface. At ground level, the plaza leads to a glass entrance lobby. The sculpture on the plaza is constructed of turbine blades from an AEP generating station. The building's parking garage is to the north and wraps around to the west. Earth mounding and extensive landscaping soften the visual impact of the garage.

2-10

2-10

CENTRAL SAFETY BUILDING

120 Marconi Boulevard
1992
Architects: Brubaker/Brandt, Columbus

The new police headquarters building opened in 1992, immediately north of the old Central Police Station. At eight stories tall and with 216,000 square feet of space, the new building is nearly three times the size of the building it replaced. The exterior is granite and limestone to complement City Hall and other buildings in the area.

The interior features a large, open two-story lobby with the police information desk as a focal point. Officers stationed there answer questions, direct visitors to specific departments, and monitor security screens and alarms. The lobby also contains glass display cases and a mini-museum area. The building has a 265-seat auditorium and a cafeteria, which is open to the public. The stone lions at the front entrance were originally placed in front of the old Central Police Station.

3

Downtown South High Street

3 DOWNTOWN SOUTH HIGH STREET

3-1

3-1
NR

OHIO NATIONAL BANK

167 South High Street
1930
Architects: Richards, McCarty & Bulford, Columbus
Neoclassical Revival

The temple form, borrowed from classical architecture, was long popular for banks because it connoted strength, permanence, and stability. The former Ohio National Bank on South High Street is a good example; like its classical predecessors, it was even built with stone bearing walls.

The building's high level of detail gives it a great deal of character. To either side of the main entrance, fluted Doric columns stand in antis (between square piers). Above the columns are a full entablature and a powerful projecting pediment. Along the north side the design is more restrained, featuring pilasters between the windows. The two-story banking lobby retains its coffered ceiling and extensive decorative ornamentation.

3-2a

3-2
NR, CR

WESTIN GREAT SOUTHERN HOTEL

310 South High Street

1897

Architects: Yost & Packard, Columbus

RENOVATION

1985

SOUTHERN THEATRE

21 East Main Street

1896

Architects: Dauben, Krumm & Riebel, Columbus

AIAC

RENOVATION

1998

Architects: Feinknopf Macioce Schappa, Columbus

The Great Southern Hotel, which contains the elegant Southern Theatre, is the most prominent building along South High Street. The 400 incorporators of the Great Southern Fire Proof Hotel Company (so named for its masonry and steel construction) included some of the city's major German businessmen, who ex-

pected the hotel to stimulate the southward development of downtown toward the city's German neighborhood.

The exterior is quite lively, with the warm red of the brick walls contrasting with the light-colored stone trim. Note the round-arched windows with brick hoodmolds and the three-story semi-engaged columns on the main elevations. When the building was rehabilitated, a new cornice was installed and wooden storefronts were constructed.

The Great Southern is the only historic downtown Columbus hotel still serving its original purpose. Go inside to see the ornate two-story lobby with its carved marble reception desk and new stained-glass skylight. Note the enormous marble Ionic and Corinthian columns. The grand ballroom has its original light fixtures, marble floors, and stained-glass windows.

The Southern Theatre, which seats 933 people, has decorative plasterwork and a round proscenium arch. Outside, observe the theater's carved stone entrance arch and colored glass transom. The oldest theater in Columbus and one of the few surviving authentic nineteenth-century theaters in America, it was designed for touring theatrical productions and later used for silent films, vaudeville, and motion pictures.

The Southern Theatre was acquired by the Columbus Association for the Performing Arts (CAPA) in 1986, and restoration work was completed in 1998. The theater is now the home of the ProMusica Chamber Orchestra, the Columbus Jazz Orchestra, and the Columbus Light Opera.

3-3

3-3
NR, CR

SOUTH HIGH STREET COMMERCIAL GROUP

328–350 South High Street
1875–1900
Italianate Commercial

RENOVATION
Circa 1978–90

Immediately south of the Great Southern Hotel are six commercial buildings that show how densely developed downtown Columbus was at the turn of the twentieth century. Best preserved are the Schlee-Kemmler Building at 328 South High, built in 1895, and the structure at 350 South High, built in 1878 as a saloon.

The Schlee-Kemmler Building's facade combines both cut sandstone and pressed sheet metal; its interior features iron columns and pressed-metal ceilings. The building at 350 South High has a particularly fine cast-iron storefront. Note the date and the manufacturer's name on the base of the storefront piers. The common scale, cornice line, and repeated features, such as the stone storefront piers, give this streetscape an attractive visual continuity.

3-4
Franklin County Courts and Administrative Complex
Both sides of South High Street between Fulton and Mound Streets

FRANKLIN COUNTY HALL OF JUSTICE

1973
Architects: Prindle & Patrick, Columbus

AIAC
FRANKLIN COUNTY MUNICIPAL COURT

1979
Architects: Prindle & Patrick, Columbus

FRANKLIN COUNTY JAIL

1970
Architects: Prindle & Patrick, Columbus

FRANKLIN COUNTY COURTHOUSE

1991
Architects: URS, Columbus; Feinknopf Macioce Schappa, Columbus

FRANKLIN COUNTY COURTHOUSE ANNEX

410 South High Street
1951
Architect: Ralph Kempton, Columbus

ADDITION
1975
Architects: Prindle & Patrick, Columbus

3-4

Franklin County's offices have traditionally been concentrated in the south end of downtown Columbus. The original 1887 courthouse was located just north of the Court House Annex before its demolition in 1974. A model of the French Second Empire–style courthouse is on display in the lobby. Along the south side of the annex are several stone columns that once framed the central entrance of the old courthouse. To the east of the annex is the county parking garage, whose lively sculptural design is a welcome relief from the usual appearance of such structures.

Most of the county functions are located on the west side of High Street in several buildings constructed over a period of nearly twenty years. The buildings exhibit a great deal of diversity of design and use of materials. However, they are all contemporary high-rise buildings that appear to be a collection of office buildings rather than a courthouse in the traditional sense.

Dorrian Commons is a handsome urban park filled with trees, sculpture, and running water. The central feature is *Oval with Points,* a large sculpture by Henry Moore, which is placed on a pedestal within a fountain that operates at intervals. The water from the fountain makes its way through the park before disappearing at the park's northern edge. This park is a popular location for alfresco lunches and midday breaks.

A new courthouse is being planned north of these existing buildings.

3-5

3-5

MIRANOVA

1 and 2 Miranova Place
2000
Architects: Arquitectonica, Miami; HKS, Dallas

A curving drive, paved in stone blocks salvaged from abandoned streets nearby, leads to this three-building complex (residential tower, office building, and parking garage) located just south of the downtown riverfront. Located on formerly underutilized land that hosted a metal salvage firm, manufacturing plants, and weeds, Miranova makes a bold statement about the future of living and working downtown.

One Miranova Place contains residential condominiums. Unusual because it is a residential building in a former industrial area, it is further distinguished by its nearly all-glass curved facade, which faces north toward downtown Columbus. An irregular pattern of recessed balconies is punched into the wall, which is topped by a parapet that curves upward from east to west. Invitations to Miranova to watch the city's riverfront fireworks on the Fourth of July are highly sought after.

The residential tower is a one-sided building, very shallow in relation to its width and with a definite "back wall" southern elevation. By contrast, 2 Miranova Place, the office building, is a four-sided rectangular structure with ribbon windows and corner glazing in black glass that contrasts sharply with the light-colored exterior masonry. Its horizontal lines contrast with the verticality of the residential tower.

The Miranova complex, which includes a multistory parking garage along the south side, is somewhat isolated from the rest of downtown Columbus. However, development plans for the Whittier Peninsula to the south include many acres of new commercial and residential construction as well as large amounts of parkland, which should place Miranova right in the middle of some of the newest development in the city.

3-6

3-6
NR, CR

CULTURAL ARTS CENTER (OLD STATE ARSENAL)

139 West Main Street
1861
Italianate

AIAO, AIAC

RENOVATION
1976
Architects: Schooley Caldwell Associates, Columbus

Despite its current title, there is no hiding this building's true character. The four octagonal towers, small windows, and forbidding brick wall eloquently testify to its original use: the storage of firearms for the state militia. Built with convict labor on the site of the state's first penitentiary, it is one of Ohio's oldest arsenals.

The Italianate style was popular in Ohio at the time of the arsenal's construction. You can see elements of this style in the tall, round-arched windows and arcaded corbel table—the row of projecting brick arches at the top of the wall.

Before entering the building, look for the cast bronze shield and eagle at the northeast corner of the perimeter wall. They are from the U.S. battleship *Ohio,* which was decommissioned in 1900.

Used for military purposes into the 1970s, the arsenal is now a model of how an older building may be adapted for new purposes. The Columbus Recreation and Parks Department offers a variety of programs in this successful center. Inside, the arsenal's original open storage spaces have become galleries and work areas, and its exposed iron columns with wood beams and joists provide a delightful setting for producing and presenting artwork in many different media.

4

Downtown East Side

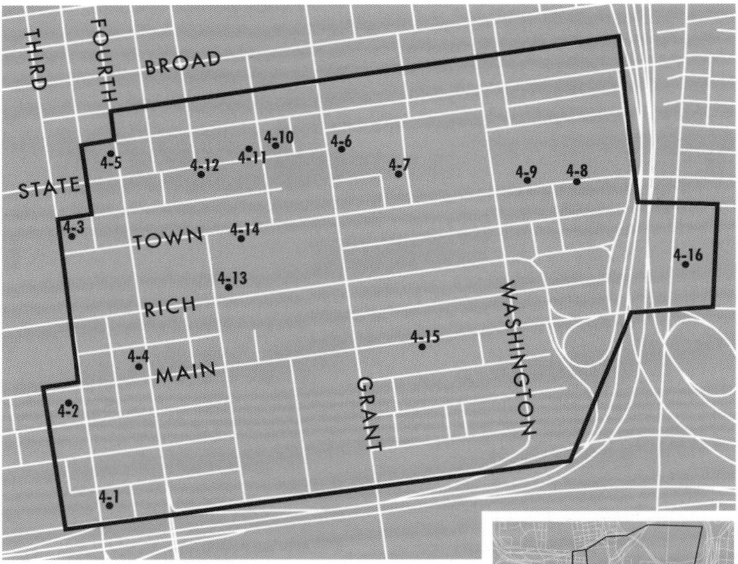

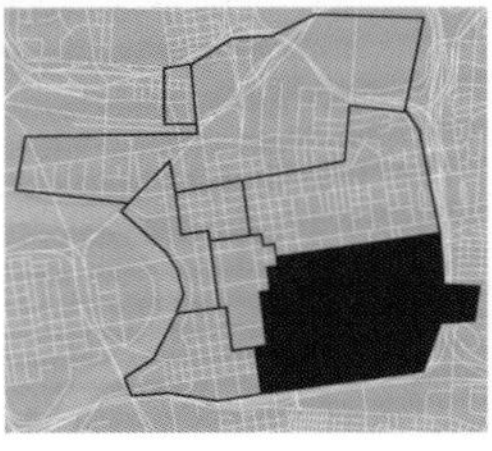

4 DOWNTOWN EAST SIDE

4-1

TRINITY EVANGELICAL LUTHERAN CHURCH (TRINITY GERMAN EVANGELICAL LUTHERAN CHURCH)

404 South Third Street

1857; steeple 1876

Romanesque Revival and Gothic Revival elements

One of the earliest of the historic downtown churches, Trinity Evangelical Lutheran is traditional in form. It has a rectangular gable roof and a symmetrical plan and elevation, with a central entrance in a buttressed projecting bay at the base of its steeple. The detailing is excellent; note the stone panel with the church's name in the central bay, and the circular stained-glass window above.

The structure rests on a high limestone foundation. Pilasters separate the brick walls into panels, each having a large segmental-arched stained-glass window with a hoodmold above. The rows of projecting arches at the tops of all walls form an arcaded corbel table, a design element common in Romanesque Revival architecture.

Built nearly twenty years after the church, the steeple has the pointed arch openings and steeply pitched roof typical of the Gothic Revival style. See how the arcaded corbel table on the main building has been reduced to a lacy decorative brickwork pattern on the steeple. The church's restrained interior features decorative capitals on the columns supporting the arch of the apse.

The church's congregation formed in 1848 after leaving the city's first Lutheran church in a controversy over the use of English for services. For many years Trinity Lutheran's services were conducted only in German.

4-2

4-2

KARLSBERGER COMPANIES BUILDING (FORD MOTOR COMPANY SHOWROOM AND GARAGE)

99 East Main Street

1918

AIAC

RENOVATION AND ADDITION

1985

Architects: Karlsberger Associates, Columbus

The winged triangular medallion on the second floor leaves no doubt about this building's original function as a Ford dealership. The front section was the showroom, with large display windows flanking the original entrance. The rear portion of the building—much more utilitarian in design—served as a garage and repair shop.

Despite its decorative brickwork, the white terra-cotta trim gives the building its distinctive character. Note its use in the storefront cornice, the window trim, the decorative panels, the Ford logo, the parapet cap, and the urns above the curved parapet.

During the 1985 rehabilitation, the owners replaced the windows and old storefront and converted the building into architectural offices. The recessed contemporary entrance includes a stylized stone winged triangle, similar to the Ford logo above it. The addition on the west side of the building was built at the same time. The large expanses of glass give it a contemporary character, while the stepped parapet on the west side of the addition echoes the decorative parapet on the facade of the original building.

4-3

4-3
CR

CENTRAL PRESBYTERIAN CHURCH (SECOND PRESBYTERIAN CHURCH)

132 South Third Street
1859
Architect: Sydney M. Stone, Connecticut
Romanesque Revival

Built of cut sandstone laid in courses, Central Presbyterian Church is especially noteworthy because of its asymmetrical design and unusual tower roofs. The church's original steeple on the north tower was nearly two hundred feet high. When an 1887 windstorm toppled the steeple, it was replaced with a concave-curved roof matching the south tower's roof.

In addition to the overall simplicity of design, you can see other features of the Romanesque Revival style: stone walls with buttresses, narrow windows with round-arched openings, and arcaded corbel tables. The church's interior has side balconies and a segmental-arched ceiling supported by braced beams resting on ornate wooden corbels. The arched stained-glass window over the west entrance came from the Von Gerichten Art Glass Company, a Columbus firm well known across the country.

Central Presbyterian's congregation dates to 1836; its members met in various locations before building this church.

4-4

4-4

HARTMAN BUILDING (HARTMAN HOTEL)

275 South Fourth Street
1898
Architects: Kremer & Hart, Columbus

AIAC

RENOVATION
2002
Architect: Jonathan Barnes Architecture & Design, Columbus

In the late nineteenth century Columbus had its own medicine man, Dr. Samuel B. Hartman. Shortly after coming to the city in 1885, Hartman started the Peruna Drug Manufacturing Company to produce the Peruna elixir he had invented. He also opened a successful hospital and sanitarium, the four-story Hartman Surgical Hotel. When that became too crowded, Hartman built this hotel nearby. The Peruna manufacturing buildings on Third Street were also close by. In 1906 Peruna was the nation's top-selling patent medicine, but Hartman's empire crumbled after a government ruling that year decreed that the potent liquid, which was as much as 25 percent alcohol, was an alcoholic beverage, not medicine.

All that remains of Hartman's Peruna empire is this six-story structure, a classic late-nineteenth-century urban hotel. The lower floors are articulated with extra ornamentation and distinctive masonry work. The hotel's most outstanding surviving feature is the large ornamented name board above the parapet. Inside, most of the room partitions have been removed, although the floors are intact.

Over the years since its use as a hotel, tenants have included the Ohio Bureau of Motor Vehicles, the Market Exchange Bank, and finally a Huntington National Bank branch. The building has been rehabilitated with commercial space on the first floor and housing on the upper floors. A new glass-and-steel stair tower is located on the west side of the building.

4-5

4-5

NR

GRISWOLD MEMORIAL YOUNG WOMEN'S CHRISTIAN ASSOCIATION BUILDING (YWCA)

65 South Fourth Street
1929
Architects: Miller & Reeves, Columbus

RENOVATION
1996
Architects: Moody•Nolan Ltd., Columbus
Second Renaissance Revival

In 1894 the Columbus YWCA opened in a house on this site. The current YWCA building was built with a $400,000 bequest from Mary J. Griswold as a memorial to her husband. The building contains residential rooms, recreational and health facilities, a chapel, and a large swimming pool on the lower level.

This eight-story structure has elements of the Second Renaissance Revival style, including stone and brick quoins at the building's corners and rusticated stone basement. The building is set on a raised foundation. The stone walls of the first and second floors are smooth-faced and bordered by rusticated quoins. Above the intermediate cornice is an iron balcony rail. The brick walls of the upper floors have brick quoins, stone window trim, and belt courses. The facade terminates in a shallow stone cornice and brick parapet. The first floor entry staircase is lined with marble, and Ionic columns decorate the lobby.

The building underwent a major renovation in 1996. Its facilities were updated to provide accommodations for 102 women, while improvements were also made in the recreational facilities, meeting areas, and administrative offices. A large reception area on the north side of the first floor and a ballroom on an upper floor are noteworthy public spaces in the building.

4-6a

4-6b

4-6

COLUMBUS METROPOLITAN LIBRARY (CARNEGIE LIBRARY)

96 South Grant Avenue
1907
Architects: Albert Randolph Ross, New York, and Wilbur T. Mills, Columbus
Beaux-Arts Classicism

CLF

RENOVATION AND ADDITION
1991
Architects: DesignGroup, Columbus

In contrast to the impressive building you see today, Columbus's public library began in 1873 as a simple reading room in City Hall, then on State Street. Andrew Carnegie's $200,000 gift to Columbus allowed the library to build a spacious and elegant building of its own in 1907. Ironically, after City Hall burned in 1921, the library temporarily housed the mayor and other city officials while they waited for completion of the new City Hall in the Civic Center.

Built of white Vermont marble on a gray granite base, the library is a bearing-wall structure. Take a minute to appreciate the library's lively facade with its carved cherubs, arches, columns, friezes, and projecting cornices. The broad frieze panels contain names, dates, and inscriptions, including a Latin inscription, "Biblioteca Fons Eruditionis," which translates as "The Library, the Fount of Learning."

A tax levy in the late 1980s paid for an addition that more than tripled the library's usable space. An atrium connects the old building and the new. As you enter the building and pass the sweeping staircases of the old, you can see the spacious new circulation area. While in the Carnegie Building, observe the coffered ceilings and barrel vaults of the main corridors. Note the cast plaster rosettes ornamenting the vaults. The dark-green columns and pilasters are done in an imitation marble known as scagliola. To sample the ambiance of the older building, climb the stone stairs to the Gallery, which is now used as an art exhibit area.

The addition at the rear of the original building now houses the library. Its marble exterior and round-arched north entrance echo design features of the original building. While its central atrium serves as an organizing feature for the spaces within, its west wall is the stone exterior wall of the original building.

Artwork by central Ohio artists is placed throughout the building. Especially notable are the two commissioned works, *Vanitas,* by Todd Slaughter, and *Life in the Blackberry Patch, 1900–1930,* by Aminah Brenda Lynn Robinson, located in the atrium of the Carnegie building and the new library atrium.

4-7a

4-7

NR, CR
OLD DEAF SCHOOL

400 East Town Street
1899
Architects: Richards McCarty & Bulford, Columbus

RENOVATION
1984
Architect: Noverre Musson, Columbus

CLF
TOPIARY GARDEN

1992
Designers: James and Elaine Mason, Columbus

TOPIARY GARDEN GATEHOUSE

1998
Architects: Sullivan Gray Bruck

The office building at the west end of the Deaf School Park was the smaller of the state school's two main buildings. This three-story brick school building has an eclectic design combining French, Gothic, Dutch, and Jacobethan elements. The two main entrances on the east side are worth a close look. Designed in a buff-colored carved stone, the entrances include floral-decorated basket-handle arches over the doorways, with an inner band of grotesque human heads. Panels above contain inspiring quotations, and the shields flanking them bear back-to-back D's reflecting the school's original name: the Institution for the Education of the Deaf and Dumb.

A larger brick residential and administration building dating from 1869 took up the north central area of today's public park. Built in the French Second Empire style, it was designed by George Bellows, Sr., father of the well-known artist.

After the state school for the deaf moved to Columbus's north side in the 1950s, these buildings housed various state offices until the late 1970s. When the larger building burned in 1981, wrecking crews very nearly demolished the school building. In the mid-1980s the city purchased the east end of the site for Deaf School Park, and the school building was privately rehabilitated as offices. Be sure to visit the park's topiary garden, where Seurat's famous painting *Sunday Afternoon on the Isle of La Grande Jatte* has been recreated using more than fifty carefully shaped yew trees.

In 1998 the City of Columbus, Motorists Mutual Insurance, and the Friends of Topiary Park contributed funds to build a gatehouse as the main entrance to the park. The 2,400-square-foot structure houses a gift shop, restrooms, and offices. Complementing the theme of the topiary garden, it was designed in brick to evoke the feeling of homes in the French countryside.

4-7b

4-8a

4-8
NR, CR

EAST TOWN STREET HISTORIC DISTRICT AND FRANKLIN AVENUE NEIGHBORHOOD

380–621 East Town Street
Franklin Avenue between Washington Avenue and Lester Drive
Circa 1850–1930

In the last half of the nineteenth century the city's elite lived on East Town Street. Business owners, political figures, and professional people built their homes here. Although considered a suburban street, East Town offered easy access by foot—or, more likely, by carriage—to the heart of downtown Columbus.

East Town Street, east of Grant to the freeway, contains a number of nineteenth- and early-twentieth-century homes and apartment buildings. Included are excellent examples of the Italian Villa, Italianate, Second Empire, Eastlake, Chateauesque, and English Revival styles. More modest late-nineteenth and early-twentieth-century homes are located along Franklin Avenue, which also retains its historic brick-paved street. The building at 382 East Town Street is a new single-family house with a historic stone facade taken from a demolished building on East State Street. At 615 East Town Street is an exuberant example of French Second Empire style.

4-8b

KELTON HOUSE

586 East Town Street
1852
Greek Revival/Italianate

RENOVATION
1978
Architect: Charles Nitschke, Columbus

Another early residence is the home built for Fernando Cortez Kelton, a local merchant. It illustrates the transition from Greek Revival to the Italianate style; note the Greek Revival entrance and wide Italianate eaves with large brackets. This house has undergone few alterations, and many of the furnishings are original, including furniture, decorative accessories, garments, and family records, making it an outstanding example of the house museum genre.

Three generations of the Kelton family resided here until the death of noted interior designer Grace Kelton, who left the home to the Columbus Foundation to be used as a museum of local history and the decorative arts. The Junior League of Columbus has restored the home to the Victorian period and offers tours and educational programs about the history of the 1850s to 1880s.

4-9

4-9

KAPPA KAPPA GAMMA HERITAGE MUSEUM

530 East Town Street
1850
Italian Villa

One of the earliest homes on East Town Street, the house was originally built for silk merchant Philip T. Snowden. During the Civil War it was the house of Governor David Tod. This is the best of several Italian Villa–style structures on the street. Style features include the central cupola (belvedere) on the roof and the decorative stone window and door trim.

Since 1942 the property has been the national headquarters of Kappa Kappa Gamma. The front portion of the house has been restored to its appearance in the 1850–60 time period and features displays depicting the history of the women's movement and the development of education for women.

State Street between Capitol Square and Grant Avenue

East State Street was primarily residential at one time, and if you look carefully you can still see some older homes. For much of the twentieth century, however, religious, institutional, and commercial buildings have taken over. Although the old residential character is largely gone, East State today remains a pleasant district of modest scale.

4-10

SALESIAN CENTER (KNIGHTS OF COLUMBUS BUILDING)

80 South Sixth Street
1927
Architects: Richards, McCarty & Bulford, Columbus
Second Renaissance Revival

Columbus Council 400 of the Knights of Columbus originally built this building as their residential club headquarters. It was designed by the same firm as the Athletic Club of Columbus. Its features included a swimming pool, gymnasium, and party rooms. The Catholic Diocese of Columbus sold the building to the Salesians of St. John Bosco, who now operate programs for central city boys and girls.

The Salesian Center is a good example of the Second Renaissance Revival style applied to a large institutional building. You can see how its five stories exhibit the traditional three-part composition of this style: base, upper floors, and cornice. Another hallmark of this style is the light-colored terra-cotta detailing, which, on the lower two floors, contrasts with the dark red brick walls. High above, the projecting cornice is also terra-cotta. Most noteworthy is the terra-cotta trim of the three center bays and the main entrance. Done in Beaux-Arts style, the trim incorporates historically accurate representations of familiar classical forms: columns, pilasters, capitals, garlands, and urns.

4-11

4-12

DOWNTOWN

4-11

FIRST SPIRITUALIST TEMPLE (WESTMINSTER PRESBYTERIAN CHURCH)

77 South Sixth Street
1857
Romanesque (Norman) Revival

First Spiritualist Temple is a very early example of a building with terra-cotta trim. Though the building was painted a few years ago, the natural reddish color of the trim is easy to spot where the paint has peeled at the round-arched doors and windows.

The church's entrance is centered in the tower; observe its medieval-looking heavy walnut doors with their massive iron strap hinges. The interior is very simple, featuring a curved apse and two rows of pews with a central aisle.

4-12

SCHOEDINGER STATE STREET CHAPEL

229 East State Street
1918
Architects: Howell & Thomas, Columbus
Spanish Mission Revival

The Schoedinger Chapel's modest size and intimate scale fit well into the streetscape of East State Street. It is the only downtown building constructed in the Spanish Mission Revival style, as can be seen in its patterned brickwork, wrought-iron window screens, and overall form and massing. The architects carried out the style even to the small bell tower extension atop the gable roof. Inside they included wrought-iron light fixtures and an ornamented wood beam ceiling.

Look closely and you will find that the chapel was built onto the front of a brick house. Constructed sometime after the Civil War, it was the home of Dr. Starling Loving, founder of Starling Medical College, which once stood where Grant Hospital is today.

4-13

4-13
NR

HOLY CROSS CHURCH, RECTORY, AND SCHOOL

204–12 South Fifth Street
1848
Architect: Cornelius Jacobs

ADDITION
1877
Architect: George H. Maetzel, Columbus
Gothic Revival

RECTORY
1860

SCHOOL
1870
Italianate

Holy Cross is the oldest church building in downtown Columbus. Its German-speaking parishioners made up the city's first Roman Catholic congregation, which formed in 1833.

You can trace this church's traditional symmetrical form from its high limestone foundation to its tall central tower and steeple (added between 1848 and 1858). Other than some sparse exterior crenellation on the parapet walls, the short spires, and the tower, the church has little ornamentation. In keeping with the Gothic Revival style, window and door openings all have pointed arches. Stone-capped buttresses divide the structural bays. Ornate painted murals decorate the interior plaster walls and ceiling. After an 1877 fire, the altar and roof were repaired and a three-story sacristy was added to the east end of the church.

Just to the north are the rectory and the school, very restrained Italianate structures. In addition to gable end walls, the rectory has a central wall dormer high above the entrance. The dormer is flanked by corbeled wing walls above an arcaded corbel table. Besides the projecting sills below, the rectangular windows have projecting decorative hoodmolds above. The L-shaped school has a shallow hipped roof.

This complex is the only survivor of urban renewal in the 1960s, when the entire surrounding neighborhood was demolished.

4-14

4-14

OHIO PUBLIC EMPLOYEES RETIREMENT SYSTEM BUILDING (OPERS)

277 East Town Street
2003
Architects: NBBJ, Columbus

From High Street to Grant Avenue, Town Street has been completely remade over the past four decades. No building along the street is more than about forty years old, and most are much newer. Dominated by the City Center retail complex at its west end and Grant Hospital at its east, for many years East Town was a street of low-rise contemporary buildings of varying designs. The hospital's Baldwin Tower, now demolished and replaced by a new pavilion, was the first high-rise structure in the area, but today the OPERS Building has a very strong presence in the streetscape.

The building has two parts: an older west portion from the 1980s and the recently completed east portion. Although they function as a single building, the two parts have notably different designs. The west portion is a low-rise structure, boxy in form and with a distinct horizontality. Its dark band windows contrast with its matte-finish stone exterior. With its generous setback, screen of trees, and sloped upper wall, it has a very subdued presence.

The new east portion, by comparison, has a much more animated design. The facade has numerous advancing and receding planes, the composition is asymmetrical, and glass constitutes a far larger part of the surface area. The main entrance is deeply recessed beneath fixed metal canopies, and the entire composition has a lightness not found in the older part of the building.

Market Exchange District

East Main Street from South Grant Avenue to Interstate 71

The Market Exchange District once encompassed the blocks immediately around the old Central Market, which stood along the west side of South Fourth Street between Town and Rich streets. The market was demolished in the 1960s, and commercial activity in the area declined for many years. Today the Market Exchange District is located farther east, primarily along East Main Street east of South Grant Avenue.

Here can be found a variety of generally low-rise new and rehabilitated buildings. Commercial activity on Main Street has increased greatly as new tenants have occupied contemporary office and restaurant space. Developers, architects, and others have found the district a convenient place to locate their offices.

4-15

4-15
AIAC

MAIN STREET GATEWAY BUILDINGS

500 and 515 East Main Street
2002 and 2004
Architects: DesignGroup, Columbus

These two buildings, located diagonally across from each other at the Market Exchange District's east end, are among the newest and largest in the area. They were designed as gateway buildings on Main Street, one of the principal approaches to downtown Columbus from the east. At 515 East Main Street is a 61,000-square-foot building with a brick skin on the north elevation and a street-level entrance; both are reminiscent of the traditional commercial architecture along the street. The design's orientation and screening capture the maximum amount of natural daylight while avoiding unwanted solar heat gain.

The building at 500 East Main Street is lower in height and smaller in scale but maintains a strong streetscape presence with its generous glazing and street-level entrances. It incorporates retail as well as office space.

Both structures have brought welcome activity to a street that had long suffered disinvestment, and they have spurred further nearby development.

4-16a

4-16b

4-16
NR

COLUMBUS DEPARTMENT OF HEALTH (OHIO INSTITUTION FOR THE EDUCATION OF THE BLIND)

240 Parsons Avenue
1874
Architect: William Tinsley, Cincinnati
French Second Empire

RENOVATION AND ADDITION
2002
Architects: DesignGroup, Columbus

This outstanding mid-Victorian structure is one of the last two state institutional buildings in Columbus (the other is the old Deaf School at 400 East Town Street). The land was purchased in 1837 for a school for the blind; this building served that purpose until the 1950s, when the school moved to the city's far north side. The building, whose construction began in 1869 as part of Governor Rutherford B. Hayes's capital building program, is the second school on the site; it replaced several 1839 buildings. Although the original building was E-shaped, several additions over the years have given it an irregular plan. The school accommodated 250 students and 60 staff members.

When the sandstone walls of this structure were going up, enthusiasm for the French Second Empire style was peaking in Ohio. Today, despite the removal of the large central and two corner towers, you can still see many hallmarks of the style, like the high mansard roofs with ornamental iron cresting, arched window openings, smooth stone corner quoins and window trim, and generally vertical proportions.

The Ohio Department of Public Safety relocated in 1998, leaving the 240,000-square-foot complex—a five-story main building and four connected buildings—vacant. The City of Columbus took over the building and renovated it for use by the Columbus Department of Health. An addition on the east side of the building now serves as the front entrance to the building and is accessible from a new parking deck. The former chapel space is available for use by the community.

5

Downtown East Broad Street

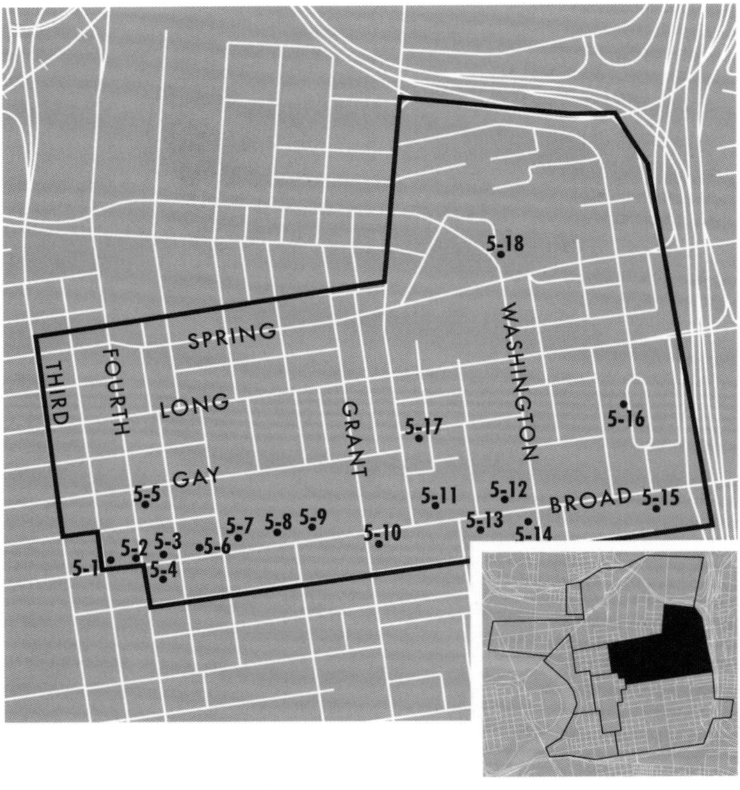

5 DOWNTOWN EAST BROAD STREET

5-1

ATHLETIC CLUB OF COLUMBUS BUILDING

140 East Broad Street
1916
Architects: Richards, McCarty & Bulford, Columbus

RENOVATION
1965
Architects: Brooks & Coddington, Columbus

Early in the twentieth century, most large cities had at least one downtown businessmen's club with sports facilities. The Athletic Club had its grand opening on January 19, 1916. The club's modest main door, centered in its Broad Street facade, contrasts markedly with this richly ornamented building, whose design strongly resembles that of a Renaissance Italian urban palace. The first and second floors form a distinct decorative unit, which contrasts with the relatively plain upper-floor walls and projecting bracketed cornice. The club's most notable design features are its large, arched second-story windows on the south (main) and west sides. The arched areas contain bas-relief shield motifs; also note the lions' heads topping the ornamental keystones. On the west side the three projecting bays added during the 1965 renovation increased the seating capacity of the main dining room. A curved staircase leads from the lobby to the second floor, where a ballroom extends across the front of the building. The ballroom's warm wood paneling and decorative painted ceiling make it one of the most elegant spaces downtown.

5-2

5-3

5-2

EMPIRE BUILDING (YUSTER BUILDING)

150 East Broad Street
1924

Despite the glitter of its entrance—note the gold-leaf clad grillwork and the decorative carving surrounding its name—the eight-story Empire Building is a good example of mid-1920s moderate-scale commercial architecture. Built against the east wall of the Athletic Club, the building is nearly square. Its first floor has five bays on the south and four on the east side. Note how the storefronts on the first floor and the office windows on the second floor are set into large segmental-arched openings with a bracketed cornice above, providing a solid visual base for the upper six floors. Pilasters divide these floors into double-window bays. Within each bay the windows are further separated by narrow pilasters. The facade terminates in a plain, low parapet rather than a projecting cornice. Renovations included installing new windows, restoring the building's marble floors, and replacing the electrical and heating/cooling systems.

5-3

BORDEN BUILDING

180 East Broad Street
1974
Architects: Harrison & Abramovitz, New York

Few downtown high-rise buildings have a plainer or more severe design than the four-by-six-bay Borden Building. Observe the powerful grid set up by the triangular-profile full-height pilasters and the flat, unadorned spandrels. The narrow band windows are dark-tinted, giving each wall a more uniform appearance than the original green-tinted glass. The dark glass also complements the natural metallic finish of the structure's walls. The setback from Broad Street creates a large plaza in front of the building.

5-4

5-4

NR

COLUMBUS CLUB (BENJAMIN SMITH HOUSE)

181 East Broad Street
Circa 1865
Architect: Nathan B. Kelly, Columbus
French Second Empire

Despite its three careers—as private residence, governor's mansion, and private club—this building is still one of the finest in Columbus and an outstanding example of the French Second Empire style. Notice how architects used cut sandstone as decorative trim for the quoins at the corners and at the entrance bay, the Corinthian columns at the entrance, and hoodmolds over doors and windows. Also observe the slate mansard roof and the round-arched double entrance doors. The interior retains its residential character, with much of its original trim and detailing. A large curving staircase dominates the central entrance hall; several rooms have high ceilings, rich woodwork, and ornate Victorian mantelpieces. The house is linked to a former carriage house at the rear of the property.

After living in the house for eighteen years, the original owner, financier Benjamin Smith, rented the home to governors George Hoadly (1884–86) and Joseph Foraker (1886–90), making this Ohio's first governor's mansion. Since Governor Foraker moved out in 1890, the building has been used exclusively by the Columbus Club.

5-5

5-5
NR

COLUMBUS ATHENAEUM (MASONIC TEMPLE)

32 North Fourth Street
1898
Second Renaissance Revival

ADDITION
1935

RENOVATION
1998
Architects: Schooley Caldwell Associates, Columbus

The Masonic Temple reflects Second Renaissance Revival design in its distinctly rusticated base and ornamented top floor, cornice, and parapet. The intervening floors are plain and largely unornamented. The Temple's strongest design elements are the three rectangular entrance arches trimmed in limestone. Even though all the upper-floor windows have been replaced, the overall character remains intact. The southern portion of the Masonic Temple, which dates to 1898, originally had a shallow gable roof. In 1935, when the Masons doubled the size of the building to 175,000 square feet, the architects concealed the roof behind an ornamented parapet wall. Also at this time, the main entrance was relocated to the center of the building. Though on first glance the building appears symmetrical, if you count the bays to the right and left of the main entrance you can see that it is not. The Temple's facilities included a cigar counter, billiards room, dining room (closed in 1993), 945-seat theater/ballroom, and 400-seat theater.

When the Masons moved their offices to the suburbs, they were unable to find a buyer for the building, and by 1995 they planned to raze the building and operate a surface parking lot on this site. However, with assistance from the Ohio Preservation Alliance, an investor group purchased the building, renamed it the Columbus Athenaeum, and undertook its renovation.

Air conditioning has been installed, electrical systems have been updated, and better accessibility for people with disabilities has been provided. The building now serves as an excellent place for meetings, conferences, wedding receptions, and parties. Special features are the Olympian Ballroom; the Priory Meeting Room, with a vaulted ceiling and murals of the Crusades; and a large theater space.

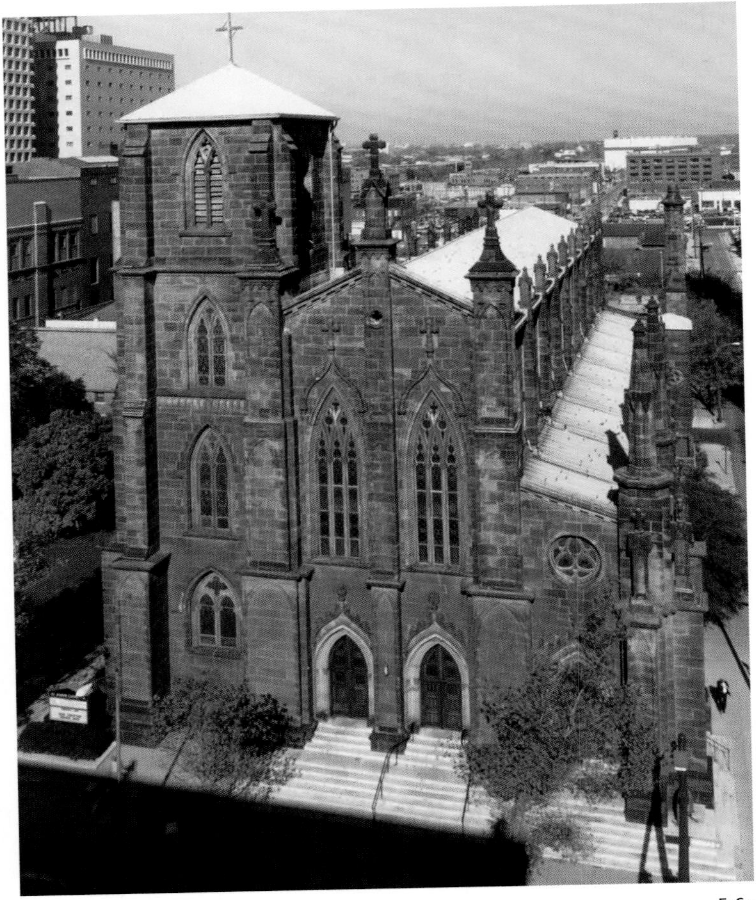

5-6a

5-6b

5-6
CR

ST. JOSEPH CATHEDRAL

212 East Broad Street
1878
Architect: Michael Harding, Columbus

RENOVATION
1914 and 1949
Architects: Richards, McCarty & Bulford, Columbus
Gothic Revival

RENOVATION
1986
Architects: Feinknopf Macioce Schappa, Columbus

BISHOP'S HOUSE, CHANCERY, AND RECTORY

1950

St. Joseph's pointed Gothic arches and aged sandstone walls bring a European feeling to East Broad Street. Asymmetrical in form, the cathedral has features one might expect to see in any continental city or town, including the pinnacles on the towers, stone buttresses supporting the side walls, and interior vaulting. The heavy tooling of the exterior stone gives the building a strong texture appropriate to its design. Its irregular plan and massing, pointed-arch window and door openings, and its liberal use of stone spires and pinnacles give the church a lively profile and make it a fine example of the Gothic Revival style. A 250-foot spire was proposed for the southwest corner but was never built. Despite the irregular exterior design, the interior is symmetrical and traditional in design. The nave has a central aisle with two side aisles and is lighted by windows in the clerestory. Clustered columns support the clerestory and roof, the columns continuing up as ribs to form groin vaults that run the length of the nave. The interior was renovated in 1986, when the new baldachino over the altar was constructed.

The bishop's residence, chancery, and rectory are stone, but not in a Gothic style. They are set back behind the lawn, west of the cathedral, creating an attractive oasis in the center of downtown Columbus.

5-7

5-7

MIDLAND BUILDING

250 East Broad Street
1971
Architects: Thomas E. Stanley & Associates, Dallas

RENOVATION
2005–6
Architects: RP Hughes, Columbus

The high contrast of its black-and-white facade gives the Midland Building a strong presence on East Broad Street. Notice how the dark glass makes the windows' mullions nearly invisible. Combining these visually solid black bands with the white pilasters gives this building a powerful verticality.

Even though it lacks a cornice or any other decorative feature, the twenty-two-story Midland reflects the traditional three-part composition of early skyscraper design. The first two floors, recessed behind an arcade of rectangular openings in the cast-masonry exterior surface, form the base, and above the segmental-arched top-floor windows, blank white walls rise to the parapet.

5-8

FRANKLIN COUNTY MEMORIAL HALL (CENTER OF SCIENCE AND INDUSTRY)

280 East Broad Street
1906
Architect: Frank L. Packard, Columbus
Neoclassical Revival

RENOVATION
1999
Architects: Maddox•NBD Architecture, Columbus

This building was originally used for public meetings and as the headquarters of the Grand Army of the Republic (GAR), a social and lobbying group of Civil War veterans. Around the turn of the century, the GAR prodded many Ohio counties into building memorial halls. Franklin County's Memorial Hall is a buff-colored brick and stone structure. Because its auditorium could seat 5,000 people, for six decades most of Columbus's major public events were held here. In 1954 Franklin County built a new Veterans Memorial across the river on West Broad Street. A decade later the Center of Science and Industry (COSI) moved into this hall, which also housed the Franklin County Historical Society. In 1973 the entrance steps were removed and the hall's front was enclosed in a tinted-glass facade to give it a more modern look.

This facade came down in 1999 during the renovation of the building after COSI moved to its new home on the western bank of the Scioto River. The building once again has its Neoclassical Revival appearance, with its entrance accentuated with six Ionic columns. Notable interior features include the entrance lobby and restored murals.

5-9

STATE EMPLOYEES RETIREMENT SYSTEM BUILDING (SERS)

300 East Broad Street
2002
Architects: DesignGroup, Columbus

As the capital of Ohio, Columbus has seen the construction of several state office buildings over the years as government has grown in size. Most of these have been clustered on or near Capitol Square, but constantly increasing space needs have pushed newer buildings farther out from the city's center. One example is the building housing the State Employees Retirement System (universally known as SERS) on East Broad Street. Constructed in part on the site of the Kelley Mansion, the home of an important early nineteenth-century political and business leader, the SERS Building adds a dramatic new facade that contrasts with its low- and mid-rise neighbors.

While clearly contemporary and innovative, the building still harks back to traditional skyscraper design, which reflects the base, shaft, and capital of the classical column. The dark stone of the SERS Building's lower floors delineates the base, while the lighter materials and repeated window patterns of the upper floors form the shaft. The classical capital is suggested by projecting screens and recessed top floors that provide a visual terminus for the composition. The screens, which appear on most floors of the building, play an important role in achieving energy efficiency by shading summer sunlight while admitting winter light.

The same architectural firm designed the addition to the State Teachers Retirement System (STRS) building across the street. A bronze sculpture with an education theme is located at the corner of East Broad and Fifth streets.

5-10

5-10

NR, CR

SENECA HOTEL

361 East Broad Street

1917

Architect: Frank L. Packard, Columbus

English Renaissance Revival

Located east of the heart of downtown, the popular Seneca Hotel was the first high-rise apartment hotel in Columbus and was considered among the city's best. Its designer, Frank Packard, was one of the premier architects in Columbus in the first quarter of the twentieth century. The hotel restaurant and ballroom were popular gathering places for much of the first half of the century.

The Seneca's design has the classic three distinct parts. The first three floors, which housed the lobby, dining room, ballroom, function rooms, and other public spaces, are clad in ornate white glazed terra-cotta. The white terra-cotta of the lower floors contrasts sharply with the next seven floors, clad in unusually dark red brick. Of the seven guest room floors, the first five are utterly devoid of ornament. The top two floors are set between projecting terra-cotta cornices and have windows in their pedimented (gabled) terra-cotta panels. This three-part exterior design is typical of early-twentieth-century high-rise buildings. Note how light wells divide the seven-story building shafts, maximizing natural light in interior spaces. The interior wood wall paneling in the lobby, the ballroom space, and the interesting balcony railings are intact.

By the mid-1960s the Seneca had lost its appeal as a hotel, and it became the women's dormitory for Nationwide Beauty Academy. After that, it served as offices for the Ohio Environmental Protection Agency from 1973 to 1987. It has been vacant for nearly two decades, and plans are now underway to convert it to apartments.

5-11

5-11
CR

FIRST CONGREGATIONAL CHURCH (UNITED CHURCH OF CHRIST)

444 East Broad Street
1931
Architects: John Russell Pope, New York City; Howard Dwight Smith, Columbus
Late Gothic Revival

ADDITION
1963
Architects: Brooks & Coddington, Columbus

Founded in 1852, this congregation occupied churches in several downtown locations before constructing the present building. John Russell Pope, the building's architect, achieved a national reputation during the early twentieth century. He was awarded the first scholarship to study at the American Academy in Rome in 1895. His architectural legacy includes Union Station in Richmond, Virginia, and the National Gallery of Art, National Archives, and Washington Monument in Washington, DC.

In the first half of the twentieth century, the Gothic Revival style was popular for church and collegiate architecture throughout the country; typically it was simpler and more solid than twelfth–fourteenth-century Gothic style. The church has a very high nave with a shallow-pitched gable roof. Substantial buttresses are set between the windows. Inside, the side aisles are very modest. High above, the church's tall, lancet-arched windows light the sides of the nave. Note the large rose window above the entrance. At the opposite end of the building, a thin copper spire tops the crossing.

5-12

5-12
NR

COLUMBUS MUSEUM OF ART (COLUMBUS GALLERY OF FINE ARTS)

480 East Broad Street
1932
Architects: Richards, McCarty & Bulford, Columbus
Second Renaissance Revival

ADDITION
1974
Architects: Van Buren & Firestone, Columbus

The museum was chartered in 1878 for the purpose of encouraging the study of the arts through creation of an art school and exhibition of works of art. The art school later became the Columbus College of Art and Design, located just to the north of the current museum. From 1919 to 1923 the art collection was housed in the Sessions House on East Broad Street. The design of the museum was reportedly influenced by the National Gallery of Art in Washington, DC, designed by John Russell Pope, who was also responsible for the First Congregational Church next door to the museum.

Set behind a broad lawn that has also become an outdoor sculpture garden, the museum is a dignified, handsome structure, a fine example of the Second Renaissance Revival style. On its completion it received considerable coverage in the art and architecture press. A projecting central block and its three large round-arched entrances dominate the front of the building. Quoins flank the entrances and are repeated along the facade. To either side of the central block are huge bas-relief friezes by Robert Aitken depicting sixty-six important artists. The entrance originally led into an open garden court that is now enclosed and covered with skylights. On the north side of the building, a 1974 addition provided a new entry from the parking lot, a gift shop, office space, and a gallery.

On the east side is a walled sculpture garden with a large reflecting pool. It was designed by Russell Page, who had an international practice based in Europe for a number of years and who is widely considered one of the most important landscape architects of the twentieth century. Many of his designed landscapes also incorporate sculpture. The garden is a popular location for special events.

5-13

5-13

FIRST CHURCH OF CHRIST, SCIENTIST

457 East Broad Street
1914
Architect: L. E. Stanhope, Chicago
Neoclassical Revival

After the architectural excesses of the late nineteenth century, many designers returned to the simplicity of classical designs. The Christian Science church is a quietly elegant structure. It sits behind a formal entrance court, back from and above the street. With its fine-grained stone exterior, the building is Neoclassical in design.

The entries on the right and left of the facade have pediments and engaged columns with Ionic capitals. The central bay is recessed behind four Ionic columns and features doorways and second-story balconies. The name of the church is inscribed in the entablature. The church's parapet has a molded stone cap.

5-14
NR

BROAD STREET UNITED METHODIST CHURCH (BROAD STREET METHODIST EPISCOPAL CHURCH)

501 East Broad Street
1885
Architect: Joseph Warren Yost, Columbus

Though widely identified as the "green stone church" on East Broad Street, this building is actually brick with a stone veneer. The stone, called serpentinite, was rarely used in central Ohio, though it was popular in the mid-nineteenth century in Philadelphia. The church's irregular massing, complex design, and extensive detail work show the eclectic influences in architecture of the late nineteenth century. Virtually all of its stone detailing is fine-grained beige sandstone. Note the tall corner tower and the decorative roofline elements and smaller towers. On the interior, the principal feature is the excellent hammerbeam roof framing, which is quite complex due to the intersecting-gable roof design.

This church was originally built as a modified Akron Plan church. The plan was developed in Akron, Ohio, in the late nineteenth century. The main feature of such a church is a large open space, or sanctuary, surrounded by Sunday school classrooms on one or two levels. The classrooms can be closed off from the sanctuary, where the main church services are held, by means of sliding or folding doors. The church's Akron Plan design has been altered, but classrooms can still be seen surrounding a central meeting hall.

5-15

5-15

FIRST BAPTIST CHURCH

583 East Broad Street
Completed 1896

One of the fine East Broad Street churches, First Baptist Church has perhaps the least traditional design. It has a gabled facade with an enormous north window that is actually a pointed-arch design, although it appears almost semicircular. The entrance arch below, done in similar proportions, reflects the shape of this window and is accentuated with bands of decorative stonework. Substantial pinnacled buttresses flank the entrance and give the facade a very solid feeling. A two-story tower is tucked behind the facade on the east elevation. The exterior stone treatment is quite unusual. The walls are primarily of smooth dressed stones whose courses are separated by narrow bands of rock-faced stone, giving the facade a horizontal-striped appearance. The building is no longer used as a church.

Jefferson Avenue and Hamilton Park Historic Districts

NR, CR

Roughly bounded by I-71, East Broad, Eleventh, and Long streets
Houses built circa 1870–1910

Before the automobile era, East Broad Street was a tree-lined parkway instead of the multilaned main artery it is today. Beginning at Capitol Square, it was a highly desirable residential area. For most of the nineteenth century and well into the twentieth, the prime city lots were on Broad Street.

Fine homes were also built just off the main thoroughfare in a development known as East Park Place. Once the site of the old state asylum, the development included Hamilton Park and Lexington and Jefferson Avenues. (Lexington was later demolished during freeway construction.) These streets were desirable because of their center landscaped medians, which increased the distance between houses on opposite sides of the street.

Hamilton Park is the better preserved of the two streets, with fewer new buildings or vacant lots. The houses are large, and most of them date from around 1890 to 1910. The buildings reflect the diversity of architectural styles popular for residential construction during this period. A number of large carriage houses have survived.

Jefferson Avenue's houses are earlier and less grand. The street has suffered from demolition of some of the original homes and the construction of new buildings, but, as in Hamilton Park, the scale and setting convey a strong sense of a turn-of-the-century neighborhood.

In 1975, the Jefferson Center for Learning and the Arts was incorporated. It includes the eight historic buildings on Jefferson Avenue between East Broad and East Long streets and is home to several nonprofit organizations related to the arts, human services, and education. Through the stewardship of the Jefferson Center, most of these homes have maintained their architectural character, and renovations are ongoing. Architect Steven Elbert designed the award-winning gazebo in the center parkway for a 1991 AIA Columbus Honor Award competition.

5-16

5-16
NR, CR

JAMES THURBER HOUSE

77 Jefferson Avenue
1873

RENOVATION
1984
Architects: Moody•Nolan Ltd., Columbus

One of the city's most significant literary landmarks is located on Jefferson Avenue: the restored home of writer James Thurber. His short story "The Night the Ghost Got In" is set here, though in the story Thurber makes the address 77 Lexington Avenue. He later said he changed the address so that he wouldn't alarm the later owners of the 77 Jefferson Avenue property. Now the "Ghost House" is a museum of Thurber memorabilia as well as a meeting place for literary events. The Writer-in-Residence Program attracts nationally known authors and journalists. In addition, the Thurber House hosts a series of literary picnics each summer that feature well-known authors reading their work. The bookstore offers books by midwestern writers and publishers.

5-17a

5-17b

5-17

Columbus College of Art & Design (CCAD)

107 North Ninth Street

AIAC

JOSEPH V. CANZANI CENTER

60 Cleveland Avenue

1993

Architects: Design Group, Columbus

AIAC

LOANN CRANE CENTER FOR DESIGN

112 Cleveland Avenue

2004

Architects: Acock Associates, Columbus

The Columbus College of Art & Design grew out of the art school once operated by the Columbus Museum of Art; today it is one of the top art schools in the United States. CCAD occupies several downtown blocks along and east of Cleveland Avenue and north of the art museum. Among its principal buildings are the Joseph V. Canzani Center (1993) and the Loann Crane Center for Design (2005), which face each other on either side of East Gay Street, east of Cleveland Avenue. Between them is perhaps the most distinctive and certainly the most visible component of the CCAD campus, the hundred-foot red metal sculpture that spells the word "art" when viewed from the east. Installed in 2001, it was designed by Artglo, a company whose president was a CCAD student in the 1960s. The sculpture is located at the heart of the campus.

5-18a

5-18
Columbus State Community College (CSCC)
550 East Spring Street

DAVIDSON HALL

1966
Architects: Moody•Nolan, Columbus

PASSAGE (PEDESTRIAN BRIDGE)

2001
Artist: L. Brower Hatcher, Providence, Rhode Island
Architects: McDonald, Cassell & Bassett, Columbus
Structural Engineers: Arup Associates, New York City

AIAC
NESTOR HALL

1992
Architects: NBBJ, Columbus

CENTER FOR TECHNOLOGY & LEARNING

2002
Architects: Maddox•NBD Architecture, Columbus

Over the past thirty years the former Columbus Technical Institute (CTI) has been transformed into Columbus State Community College. Located on cleared land just inside the northeast corner of the Innerbelt freeway, CTI took shape in the late 1960s and early 1970s in the area north of East Spring Street and east of

5-18b

Cleveland Avenue. Today, however, the CTI buildings have been augmented by new structures to handle a much greater number of students, and the campus has become part of the state's community college system.

A large parking garage occupies the east side of North Washington Avenue. At the northeast corner of Washington and East Long Street is a memorial sculpture of Columbus folk artist Elijah Pierce, whose 1954 barber shop stood on land now occupied by the garage.

North of the garage, on the north side of East Spring Street, the main campus buildings—Davidson Hall, Nestor Hall, and the Center for Technology and Learning—are a series of convex and concave curves. All have simple punched openings and very modest ornamentation. One whimsical element is the bright red curving pedestrian bridge called *Passage,* a space-frame structure that crosses Spring Street to connect the garage with Davidson Hall.

CSCC is in an area of considerable educational activity. Just to the north, beyond the freeway, is the Fort Hayes Metropolitan Education Center, while to the south is the Columbus College of Art & Design.

6

Downtown North High Street

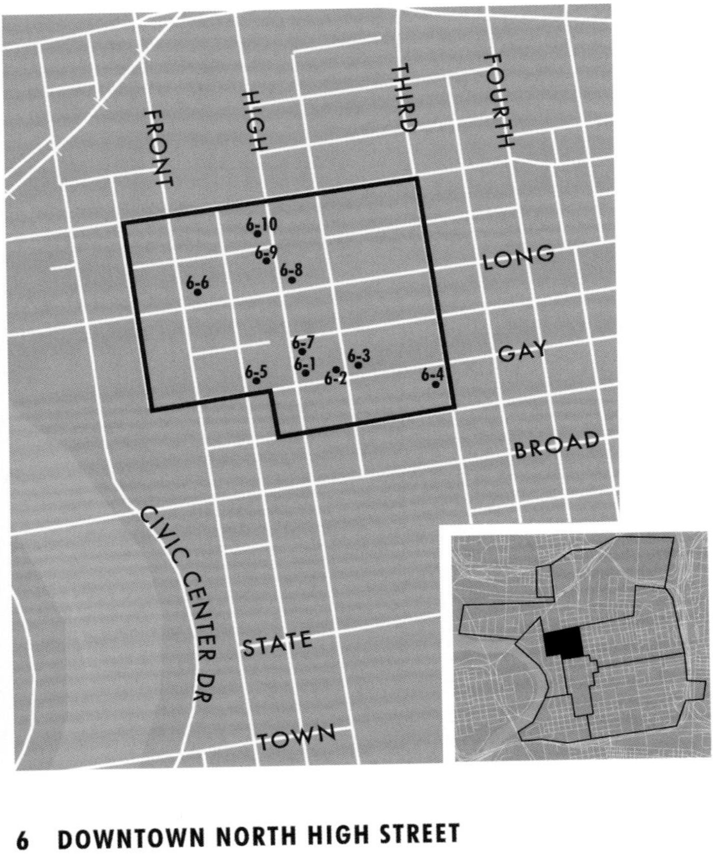

6 DOWNTOWN NORTH HIGH STREET

6-1

6-1

OLD COLUMBUS DISPATCH BUILDING

68 North High Street
1910
Architect: attributed to H. A. Linthwaite, Columbus
Second Renaissance Revival

Until 1925, this narrow (twenty-three-feet-wide) five-story building housed the *Columbus Dispatch,* the city's daily newspaper since 1871. An 1889 building of similar size on the same site housed the paper until 1907, when it burned down.

In spite of the building's modest scale, the buff-colored Bedford limestone exterior, rusticated first floor, carved features such as balustrades, pilasters, capitals, and pediments, and other decorative elements give the building a solid presence on North High Street. Note the bas-relief globes, located above the third-floor windows, that depict the newspaper's worldwide coverage.

The building has housed numerous commercial tenants since the *Dispatch* moved to its current home on Capitol Square.

East Gay Street from High to Third Streets

Circa 1880–1930

This section of East Gay Street is the only downtown street with an intact streetscape for most of its length. Though some buildings have been altered, only the one at the northwest corner of Gay and Third has been removed. Interrupted only by Pearl Alley, this segment of Gay Street has a common setback with side-by-side buildings, presenting a continuous line of building facades on both sides of the street. As a result, the street retains a cohesiveness, density, and sense of historical continuity difficult to find elsewhere in the downtown area.

This traditional streetscape contrasts with much of the contemporary development in downtown Columbus, where buildings generally stand alone, separated from adjacent structures by plazas or other open space. Observe the great variety in building design and detailing that gives this portion of Gay Street much of its character.

6-2

RUGGERY BUILDING

20–24 East Gay Street
Circa 1895
Romanesque elements

RENOVATION
2000
Architect: Jonathan Barnes Architecture & Design, Columbus

The first two floors of this eight-story brick structure, located on the north side of Gay Street next to the former Columbus Dispatch Building, feature rusticated stone pilasters, while the next five floors have windows set into three tall arches. The top floor is sandwiched between an intermediate cornice and the large building cornice at the top of the facade.

The renovation of the building resulted in the reopening of windows that had been downsized, renovation of the original lobby area, and repair of the brick and limestone exterior.

6-3

BUCKEYE BUILDING (BUCKEYE BUILDING & LOAN COMPANY BUILDING)

36–38 East Gay Street
Circa 1926

Across Pearl Alley from the Ruggery Building, this thirteen-story structure is built in the traditional early skyscraper design: a distinctive base and cornice with fairly plain office floors in between. The two-story row of engaged Corinthian columns on the first floor is its main feature. The interior has an elegant multistory banking lobby finished with classical detailing.

6-4

LAW AND FINANCE BUILDING (OHIO STATE SAVINGS ASSOCIATION BUILDING)

85 East Gay Street
1927
Architects: Simons, Britain & English, Pittsburgh
Art Moderne

Completed the same year and in the same style as the Lincoln LeVeque Tower, this building is also a good example of the Art Moderne style. The architect combined three materials in the building's traditional three-part early-skyscraper design: Litholite, a cast stone material, covers the three-story base. The upper seven floors are clad in brick; above them the parapet wall ornamentation, resembling a necklace of spark plugs, is made of polychrome (multicolored) terracotta. The two-story penthouses atop the north and south sides of the building have similar ornamentation.

The building's original ornate banking lobby on the first floor now houses a restaurant. The decorative ceiling, which features large beams constructed in plaster to look like wood, is intact. The main entrance and elevator lobby on Gay Street, a rich blend of polished brass and pale pink marble, is intimate in scale and features a handsome open stairway.

6-5

6-5
NR

RANKIN BUILDING

22 West Gay Street
1911, 1930
Neoclassical Revival

This building was confidently hailed as "the first absolutely fireproof building in the State of Ohio"; ads guaranteed that "no wood was used . . . not a carpenter was employed." Although it is still fireproof, today it looks entirely different than it did in 1911, when it was built to house Buckeye State Building and Loan. Its original design was typical of buildings of the period, with an offset entrance, upper-floor offices, and a restrained cornice.

By 1930, when Union Building Savings and Loan moved in, the building was modified to have a classical stone facade. The Neoclassical Revival style was popular for banks and public buildings because it conveyed a sense of refinement and stability. Note the design elements of the style: the simplicity and massive proportions of its two-story entrance arch, the rigid symmetry of the portico and three-story columns, and the substantial entablature above the Ionic columns.

6-6

NR

YOUNG MEN'S CHRISTIAN ASSOCIATION BUILDING (YMCA)

40 West Long Street
1924
Architects: Shattuck & Layer, Chicago
Jacobethan Revival

RENOVATION
1994
Architects: Lusk & Harkins, Columbus

The YMCA's castle-like effect is achieved through the use of stone detailing and a lively roofline silhouette. Note especially the crenellations at the second story above the main entrance and along the roofline of the north and west elevations. In addition to these features, the main facade combines two hallmarks of Jacobethan Revival style: complex brickwork and cut-stone details. The contrast between the dark red brick and light-colored cut stone enhances the three-dimensional effect of the facade. The architect, Walter F. Shattuck, designed many YMCAs in the early 1900s both in the United States and abroad.

Founded in 1855, the YMCA opened its second location in 1893 on Capitol Square. This building, the Y's third headquarters in Columbus, was opened in 1924. It cost $850,000 to build and was hailed as "the largest YMCA in the world" in the *Columbus Dispatch*. The building, which has 400 rooms, underwent a major $15 million renovation that provided air conditioning, expanded fitness facilities, and restored the original lobbies.

6-7

WHITE-HAINES BUILDING (C. O. HAINES OPTICAL COMPANY BUILDING)

82 North High Street
1913
Architects: Richards, McCarty & Bulford, Columbus

The White-Haines Building's concrete frame permitted the use of unusually large windows in its three-bay facade. There are relatively small amounts of masonry between the windows. Note how much smaller the windows are in nearby masonry bearing-wall buildings.

The light-colored glazed terra-cotta exterior forms a grid of narrow projecting pilasters and horizontal spandrels between floors. The recessed rectangular spandrel panels have trefoil or cloverleaf-shaped forms, strongly reminiscent of English designs from the early nineteenth century. The cornice also carries out this leaf motif. The north storefront is constructed of finely detailed bronze-colored metal, a fitting design for the fine jewelry store that was once located here.

6-8
NR

ATLAS BUILDING (COLUMBUS SAVINGS AND TRUST BUILDING)

8 East Long Street
1905
Architect: Frank L. Packard, Columbus
Second Renaissance Revival

RENOVATION
1982
Architect: David C. Hughes, Columbus

Originally built at a cost of $500,000, this skyscraper has some of the most exuberant terra-cotta ornamentation in downtown Columbus, and it is probably the city's best remaining example of decorative terra-cotta.

Remarkably narrow for its length, the building measures five by fifteen bays. As a result, its visual impact varies depending on whether you are looking at its west or its south side, as the north and east sides are very plain and unadorned. The architectural composition is classic early skyscraper: a very distinct three-floor base, seven floors of very plainly detailed windows, and three heavily decorated upper floors. The huge cornice is remarkable for its height, projection, and dominating elements, such as the brackets. The first three floors are of dark red rusticated stone, as are the columns at the main entrance. Several years ago the storefronts were skillfully rehabilitated using precast colored concrete.

6-9

6-9

BRUNSON BUILDING

145 North High Street
1905
Architect: Charles A. Stribling, Columbus
Commercial

RENOVATION
2005
Architect: Jonathan Barnes Architecture & Design, Columbus

At the turn of the twentieth century, the Brunson Building's steel frame, relatively large windows, and imposing twelve stories made it a very modern building. Today it illustrates the transition between the large masonry bearing-wall buildings of the nineteenth century and the glass-clad steel-framed skyscrapers of the twentieth.

The Brunson has a simplicity of design: its windows almost completely lack ornamentation, and its simple brick cornice projects only slightly. Compare the Brunson with the nearby Atlas Building at the corner of High and Long streets. Built at the same time, the Atlas is much more heavily ornamented.

Following a trend in downtown Columbus, the building has been converted into residential condominiums. A contemporary tower, with glass and aluminum as the predominant exterior materials, has been added to the north side of the building to accommodate this new use.

6-10
NR, CR

LARRIMER BUILDING (COLUMBIA BUILDING; CLOCK RESTAURANT)

161–67 North High Street
Circa 1890
Architects: Stribling & Lum

RENOVATION
1980
Architects: Schooley Caldwell Associates, Columbus

This structure is unusual in several ways. First, it is a partial building, having lost two upper floors. Second, and more obvious, are its rare yellow sandstone facade and striking storefront. Third, a restaurant occupies the historic saloon space, continuing more than a century in this use.

Joseph and William Bott built the ornate storefront about 1898 at another location on High Street and moved it to the Larrimer Building about 1905. As advertised on the storefront, Bott Brothers offered cigars and billiards as well as drinks and meals in their bar and restaurant. This space has survived largely intact in the front portion of the building. Unique features include the mahogany bar, back bar, mosaic tile floor, and ornate ceiling, which are all original.

7

Downtown North Innerbelt

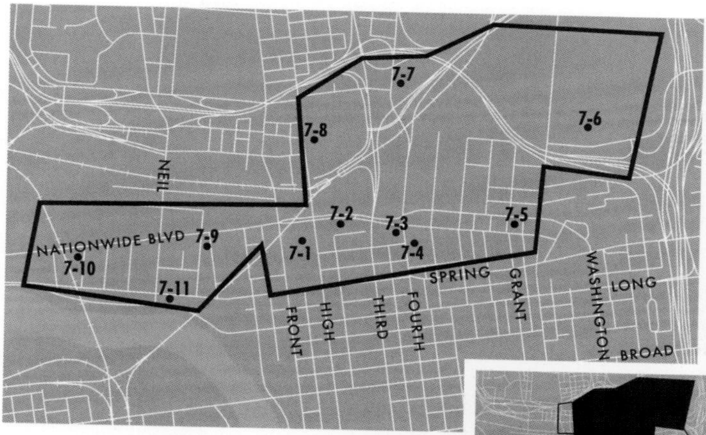

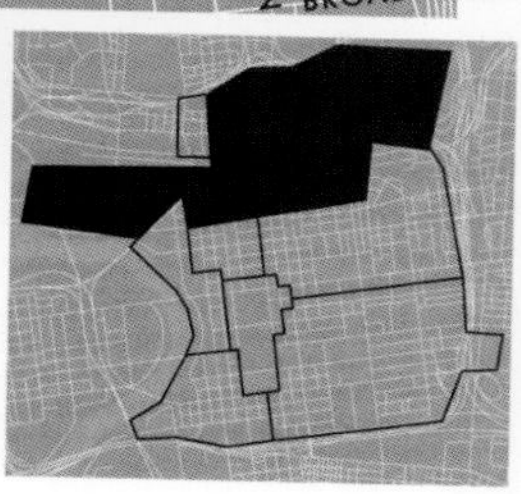

7 DOWNTOWN NORTH INNERBELT

7-1a

7-1b

7-1

Nationwide Plaza

Bounded by North High Street, West Spring Street, North Front Street, and Nationwide Boulevard

ONE NATIONWIDE PLAZA

1978

Architects: Harrison & Abramovitz, New York City; Brubaker/Brandt, Columbus

THREE NATIONWIDE PLAZA

1989

Architects: NBBJ, Columbus

WILLIAM GREEN OHIO BUREAU OF WORKERS' COMPENSATION BUILDING

1989

Architects: NBBJ, Columbus; Patrick + Associates, Columbus

PLAZA

Landscape Architects: Sasaki Associates, Boston

This area of North High Street has been completely remade into a high-density office complex. Previously, small commercial buildings, warehouses, and the Chittenden Hotel occupied this land. The moving force behind the transformation of the area was Nationwide Insurance Companies.

One Nationwide Plaza, Nationwide's headquarters building on High at Nationwide Boulevard, opened in 1978 and was the first significant skyscraper to be constructed at the north end of downtown. Set at an angle to the street, the building is striking for its scale and simplicity of design.

Immediately south of One Nationwide Plaza are two other high-rise buildings, completed in 1989. Three Nationwide Plaza and the Ohio Bureau of Workers' Compensation have complex building forms and surfaces. With stepped-back facades and profiles, they add visual interest to the skyline.

The most distinctive feature of this grouping is the landscaped plaza and the interior public areas that connect the buildings. The outdoor plaza is built at several levels. Moving water, sculpture, and plantings integrated into the design result in an inviting green oasis downtown. Connecting all three buildings is an enclosed atrium featuring large tropical plants and a series of fountains and waterfalls.

7-2

Nationwide Boulevard Warehouses

55–89 East Nationwide Boulevard

Completed 1882–1922

55 EAST NATIONWIDE BOULEVARD

NR, AIAO, AIAC

RENOVATION

1983

Architects: Böhm-NBBJ, Columbus

77 EAST NATIONWIDE BOULEVARD

CLF

RENOVATION

1984

Architects: Trott & Bean, Columbus

89 EAST NATIONWIDE BOULEVARD

Originally these three structures looked north to Columbus Union Station and the Pennsylvania Railroad Produce Yard, which fronted along Naghten Street. Construction of the Greater Columbus Convention Center and the Hyatt Regency Hotel, along with other redevelopment, have radically changed what was the middle of the city's warehouse and wholesale district, which began west of Front Street near the Ohio Penitentiary site and extended eastward along Naghten Street and Mt. Vernon Avenue to about Cleveland Avenue.

Today these former warehouses give some idea of this district's early architecture. The five-story brick bearing-wall structure at 55 East Nationwide was built in 1882 as a warehouse for the Columbus Transfer Company. The company added the eastern half of the building around 1900. Note the complex decorative brickwork in its arched windows and its parapet wall, as well as the light-colored stone sparingly used as trim. The west side windows and new storefronts were added when the building was rehabilitated in the early 1980s as offices and again nearly 20 years later into a loft-style hotel.

The two-story warehouse at 77 East Nationwide was built in 1922. Note how the design of this type of building changed between the 1880s and the 1920s. It is a simple building, horizontal in form and without ornamentation or decorative brickwork found on its neighbor to the west. This warehouse originally had first-floor storefronts and large windows on the second floor. During its con-

7-2

version to office space, however, each bay was expanded into a single large glazed opening with an applied metal grid reminiscent of historic architectural forms.

The former Amicon Warehouse at 89 East Nationwide was built as a produce warehouse around the turn of the century. Because it needed a minimum of natural light, it had only a few extremely narrow arched windows on the second and third floors. During its rehabilitation as restaurant and office space, much larger windows were created. The arched openings on the first floor are original, but have been reglazed. Ornamentation is limited to some projecting brick courses on the parapet.

Other early-twentieth-century warehouses nearby have also been rehabilitated for new uses. One group is along Chestnut Street between High and Fourth Streets, and another is along North Fifth Street between Spring and Naughten.

7-3
NR, CR

FLATIRON BUILDING (H. A. HIGGINS BUILDING)

129 East Nationwide Boulevard
1914
Designer and builder: Herbert Aloysius Higgins, Columbus

This is downtown's only flatiron building. H. A. Higgins built the triangular structure to fit an odd-shaped piece of land in what was once the heart of the city's warehouse and wholesale district. As it does now, the first floor has probably always housed a saloon or similar enterprise.

Although very plain, this building does have some decorative features. Study the craftsmanship of the brickwork, such as in the pointed-arch windows on the first floor. The walls are laid in patterns to create recessed and projecting panels, window and door arches, and a projecting cornice. Contrasting with the red brick is the light-colored stone ornamentation. Look for the stone belt courses, keystones, and window sills and the parapet cap at the top of the building.

DOWNTOWN

7-4

7-4
NR, CR

CENTRAL OHIO FIRE MUSEUM (ENGINE HOUSE NO. 16)

260 North Fourth Street
1908

CLF

RENOVATION
1989–2000
Architects: Schooley Caldwell Associates, Columbus

Former Engine House 16 is one of the city's most ornate and best-preserved old fire stations. Originally designed for horse-drawn steam engines, it was modified as times and needs changed. The firehouse became Station 1 in 1952 and was finally retired from service in 1984.

The building now has a new life as the Central Ohio Fire Museum. In 1989–90 exterior renovation returned the firehouse to its original appearance with reconstruction of the decorative hose tower and the Flemish gable parapet on the facade. The interior was renovated a decade later to house historic firefighting equipment and educational displays about the Columbus Fire Department and fire safety. Columbus firefighters have contributed funds through payroll deductions over many years to make the vision of this museum a reality.

7-5

7-5

ST. PATRICK CHURCH

280 North Grant Avenue
1853; 1936

PARISH HALL

2004
Architects: Harper Architects & Engineers, Columbus

St. Patrick's was the first English-speaking Roman Catholic congregation in Columbus, and this is one of the oldest surviving churches in downtown.

The church sits on a high cut limestone foundation. Observe how the two square crenellated towers with arched openings dominate the austere facade. Projecting slightly from a wall inset between the towers, the entrance features a pointed arch opening and heavy wooden doors. Buttresses with stone caps are located between the stained-glass window openings on the north and south elevations. When a fire destroyed all but the exterior walls in 1935, parishioners rebuilt the church with a new roof and interior in 1936.

As part of a major expansion project, a parish hall was constructed and connected to the church with a new entrance lobby. The parish hall features a brick exterior with pilasters separating the bays, stone trim, and wide overhanging bracketed eaves. An interior landscaped courtyard provides natural daylight to all of the interior spaces. The interior of the church was also renovated as part of the project.

7-6a

7-6b

7-6
NR

Fort Hayes Metropolitan Education Center
Fort Hayes USAR Center (United States Arsenal)

Bounded by CSX tracks, Interstate 71, Interstate 670, and Cleveland Avenue

SHOT TOWER

1864
Italianate

RENOVATION
1980

BUILDING 110 RENOVATION

1992
Architects: Moody•Nolan Ltd., Columbus

HISTORIC HIGH SCHOOL BUILDINGS RENOVATION

2006
Architects: Schooley Caldwell Associates, Columbus

ARTS IMPACT MIDDLE SCHOOL

2006
Architects: Karlsberger Companies, Columbus

CAREER CENTER BUILDINGS RENOVATION

2007
Architects: DesignGroup, Columbus

Fort Hayes is both a modern education center and a military institution with roots going back to the Civil War. It is Ohio's oldest federal military installation in continuous use. In 1863 the state gave a tract of land known as Neil's Woods to the federal government, which promptly built an arsenal to serve Ohio Civil War regiments. At the main arsenal building, troops manufactured and repaired weapons and prepared ammunition. Known as the Columbus Barracks after the Civil War, the seventy-seven-acre site was active during the Spanish-American War and World War I. Renamed Fort Hayes in 1922 to honor Ohio-born President

7-6c

Rutherford B. Hayes, it was a reception center for new recruits during each major war. Today the U.S. Army maintains a small presence at Fort Hayes.

The 1864 Shot Tower still dominates the site. This brick three-story structure, which measures about 60 by 180 feet, has a powerful, simple Italianate design, with large windows and a large arched entrance in the base of the tower. Its central stair tower is 32 by 36 feet. Despite its current name, the building did not serve as a shot tower (defined as a tall structure in which molten lead was poured into water to form spherical bullets). The building houses an art gallery on the first floor and classrooms and offices throughout.

Today the Fort Hayes campus accommodates three separate Columbus public school buildings: an arts-impact middle school, an arts-oriented high school, and a career center. The site incorporates a number of other historic buildings, including three along the western edge of the campus, the former administration building immediately north of the Shot Tower, and the former commandant's house on the east side. Rehabilitation of several of these long-vacant buildings has provided additional classroom space. Other buildings completed between 1870 and the 1920s on the site are awaiting new uses.

7-7

7-7

SMITH BROTHERS HARDWARE COMPANY BUILDING

580 North Fourth Street
1926

AIAC, CLF

RENOVATION
1999
Architects: Moody•Nolan Ltd., Columbus

Smith Brothers was a wholesale hardware company that closed in the mid-1980s. The building was vacant for nearly fifteen years before being renovated and converted into offices. It is an excellent example of poured-concrete frame construction, a method that allows large windows in the brick walls because the walls are not load-bearing. Ornamentation is confined to the main entrance on Fourth Street. During renovation a new entrance was added on the south side of the building. Interior work took advantage of the large open spaces and the rows of mushroom-shaped supporting columns to create loft space. The classic industrial water tower and the Smith Brothers name were retained and make the building a visual landmark from both downtown and the I-670 freeway.

7-8
Greater Columbus Convention Center Complex

North High Street and Nationwide Boulevard area

HYATT REGENCY HOTEL

AIAC
350 North High Street
1980
Architects: Prindle & Patrick, Columbus
Brutalist

OHIO CENTER

350 North High Street
1980
Architects: Godwin Böhm NBBJ, Columbus
Contemporary

GREATER COLUMBUS CONVENTION CENTER

CLF
400–500 North High Street
1993
Architects: Peter Eisenman, New York City; Richard Trott & Partners, Columbus
Deconstructivist

CONVENTION CENTER ADDITION

2000
Architect: Karlsberger Companies, Columbus

Standing on the former site of Columbus's Union Station is the city's principal convention complex, which includes the Hyatt Regency Hotel and the former Ohio Center. The hotel anchors the site, with the convention facilities located to its north and east. It is a mix of recent architecture styles.

The 631-room Hyatt hotel might be described as the epitome of Brutalist architecture: a huge black glass block has been set on two stout concrete legs. The building is set at an angle to High Street and reinterprets the treatment of One Nationwide Plaza across the street.

The hotel is connected directly to the Ohio Center, which includes Battelle Hall (a combination arena and exhibition hall with 6,000 permanent seats and

7-8

90,000 square feet of floor space) and a variety of specialty shops and restaurants. A restored mural, *Music,* by Columbus artist Emerson Burkhart is located above the Regency Ballroom and Battelle Hall space. Originally painted for Central High School in 1934, it was removed prior to the conversion of that building into the Center of Science and Industry.

North of the Hyatt and Ohio Center is the Greater Columbus Convention Center. This building's design, the winner of an international competition funded by the Limited, Inc., in 1988, is the work of Peter Eisenman and Richard Trott, the same team responsible for the Wexner Center at Ohio State University. Eisenman and Trott designed the new convention center complex as five colorful forms clad in corrugated metal and in varying heights and widths. Seen from above, these twisting forms reflect the railroad tracks that were once on this site. The North High Street facade is made of brick, metal, and precast concrete broken down into a number of distinct blocks intended to mirror the proportions of the historic brick buildings across the street.

Inside the convention center are fifty-four meeting rooms as well as a 25,000-square-foot ballroom. To the rear of the building is the 216000-square-foot exhibition hall. The Greater Columbus Convention Center has been such a success that within six years after its completion an addition was needed. The addition to the north continues the pastel exterior colors and simplifies the forms of the original design.

Arena District

7-9

CLF

Bounded by Spring Street, North Front Street, Neil Avenue, and I-670

The northwestern part of downtown Columbus was once a district of warehouses, wholesalers, light industry, and various commercial enterprises. Bounded to the north and south by main railroad lines, the area was laced with spur tracks serving numerous businesses. It was a busy, hard-working district full of trains and trucks and delivery vehicles that fed the commerce of the city. In the southwest quadrant stood the high stone wall and brooding presence of the Ohio Penitentiary. Over time, as warehousing and wholesaling moved out of the center city, the buildings either were retro-fitted for new uses or were demolished. In the 1970s one of them became the Waterworks, one of the earliest of the "theme" restaurants in Columbus, which seated patrons in old bathtubs and celebrated the city's municipal water system (the restaurant and the building today are long gone). In the 1990s a former plumbing warehouse became the Lofts, part of a hotel east of High Street. In this same period several warehouses along Marconi Boulevard were converted to offices. These buildings are still standing.

The Ohio Penitentiary did not fare so well. Despite preservationists' assessment that at least some of the "Pen" was sound enough to reuse—and worthy of it for its history and architecture—the entire complex, which dated to the 1830s, was demolished by the City of Columbus in the late 1990s. However, in contrast to many other cases of preemptive demolition that resulted in nothing more than vacant land for years after, something actually did happen. On former Pen land and in the surrounding warehousing area, the real estate arm of Nationwide Insurance began to realize its dream of a hockey arena for the city's new NHL expansion team, to

7-9a

be surrounded by a newly revitalized district of shops, restaurants, offices, and residences.

The Arena District that resulted is a good example of the best kind of New Urbanism—the recovery and revitalization of lost urban fabric. In an area of underutilized and vacant buildings, peppered with parking lots and empty land, new urban space has been created. The Nationwide Arena and associated projects in the northern part of the district have skillfully reconstructed the area's streets and lined them with offices, restaurants, and apartments. At the very beginning of the project, real estate officials of Nationwide Insurance stated that the overall design character of the district would be inspired by the industrial and warehouse architecture that had predominated there, particularly the Ohio Moline Plow Company Building.

7-9b

UNION STATION ARCH (UNION STATION ARCADE)

NR
1897
Architects: Daniel Hudson Burnham & Company, Chicago

REBUILT IN ARCH PARK
1980

MOVED TO McFERSON COMMONS
1999
Landscape Architects: MSI, Columbus
Architects: Schooley Caldwell Associates, Columbus
Beaux-Arts Classicism

Between 1850 and 1977 three different railroad depots stood at the northeast corner of High and Naughten Streets, currently the site of the Greater Columbus Convention Center and Hyatt Regency Hotel. The arch is all that remains of the last of the depots, Columbus Union Station.

The Union Station arch, part of a terra-cotta entrance arcade on North High Street, stood in front of the station itself. When demolition of the arcade began in 1976, a citizens' group saved the arch from destruction and then moved it into storage. It was later rebuilt it in a new city park at 100 West Hickory Street set aside for that purpose. The arch has since been moved from its home of nearly twenty-five years to be the gateway to McFerson Commons in the Arena District.

Designed by architect Daniel Burnham, the chief architect of the 1893 World's Columbian Exposition in Chicago, the terra-cotta arcade and the brick station reflected the Beaux-Arts Classicism that swept the nation after the Exposition. The hallmark of this ornate French style, and the dominant feature of the arch, is the use of paired columns. Another Beaux-Arts feature is the complexity of ornamentation, which leaves no surface untouched.

NATIONWIDE ARENA

200 West Nationwide Boulevard
2000
Architects: Heinlein+Schrock, Kansas City; NBBJ, Columbus

Nationwide Arena is the principal structure in the district, and its heart. Built as the home of the Columbus Blue Jackets hockey team, the arena is a major venue in the city, used to host many kinds of events. The masonry walls, large windows, and exposed steel elements of the arena are nods to the warehouse and industrial architecture that once prevailed in the Arena District, although they are blended into a clearly contemporary design. Most notable is the 135-foot light beacon at the building's east end.

The building blends well into the streetscape and is set back from Front Street behind a large public plaza. The plaza accommodates large crowds during special events and provides an urban amenity for those who live and work in the district.

7-10

OHIO MOLINE PLOW COMPANY BUILDING

NR
383 North Front Street
1913

AIAC
RENOVATION
1999
Architects: NBBJ, Columbus

The Ohio Moline Plow Company was a subsidiary of the Illinois enterprise that became a major supplier of farm machinery in the early twentieth century. The company's Front Street building was built as a sales and parts supply facility for the central Ohio area, and later served as a drug wholesaler's warehouse. When Nationwide Insurance began planning for the new Arena District in the late 1990s, the Ohio Moline Plow Building was the first to be finished, and it set the design tone for the rest of the district. The building was listed in the National Register of Historic Places for its architecture, an early example of all-masonry "fireproof" construction. Its interior has the rows of mushroom-shaped concrete columns that typified early-twentieth-century warehouses, and it has kept its working-class character intact during its conversion to restaurant and office uses.

Arena District West

7-10

Bounded on the north by Norfolk Southern Railroad Tracks, south by the Scioto River, east by Neil Avenue, west by the Olentangy River

West of the Arena District is an area that was the location of some of the city's larger close-in heavy manufacturing plants. These included the Jaeger Machine Company, a manufacturer of concrete mixers whose former office building still stands on West Spring Street just east of the Olentangy River; the Columbus Buggy Works, which is being reborn today as an office/artspace/residential complex; the city's Municipal Light Plant; the Union Fork and Hoe Company, which until recently made hand-forged steel garden implements with wooden handles; and the Belmont Casket Company. Once a lively area full of trucks and trains and manufactured goods, Arena District West went through a long period of decline and then rediscovery. Early investors who had faith in the value and character of the old industrial buildings there have now been vindicated as the Arena District's success pushes development farther and farther westward.

7-11a

7-11b

7-11

NORTH BANK PARK

Spring/Long streets at Neil Avenue
2005
Architects: Acock Associates, Columbus
Landscape Architects: MSI, Columbus

North Bank Park occupies a former no-man's-land on the Scioto riverbank across from the demolished Ohio Penitentiary. The park is a welcome oasis and a focal point for recreational activities, part of an ongoing program by the city to increase urban parkland along the river. On the site of a former pumping station, a new public pavilion built of glass, steel, and brick provides space for restrooms, events, maintenance storage, and shelter from the weather. Terraces and ramps allow access to paths along the water, and the many young trees will provide shady areas for sitting and picnicking. The pavilion reflects the utilitarian designs of the factory and warehouse buildings that occupied much of the surrounding area. This same design inspiration has helped shape new development in the Arena District just north and east of the park. In the median between Spring and Long streets, note the interpretive plaques that tell the story of the development of the area. This park affords one of the most dramatic views of the Columbus skyline.

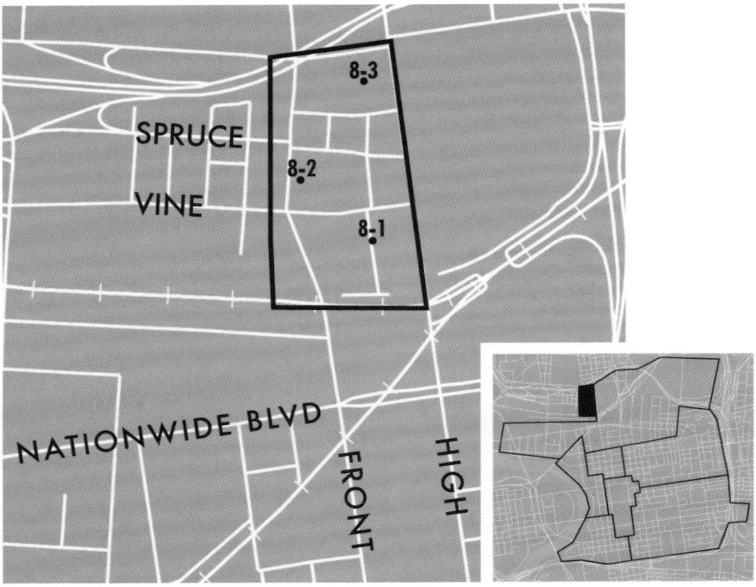

8 NORTH MARKET HISTORIC DISTRICT

8

North Market Historic District

8-1

NR, CR

The North Market Historic District occupies several blocks around the market between North High Street and Neil Avenue (within easy walks to north and south are the Short North and the Arena District, respectively). Numerous older structures, most of them former wholesale and retail buildings, still stand in the North Market Historic District. At the southeast corner of Vine and North Front is a former warehouse known as the Battleship Building because of its unusual design of steel plates riveted over a steel frame. To the east, along North High Street's west side, are the Carlile and Yankee Trader buildings, located at 445–47 and 463 North High, respectively. The Carlile has a pressed-brick facade with stone trim and has been rehabilitated as restaurant space, while the Yankee Trader has an unusual two-story front as well as a rear storefront. Its stock-in-trade is costumes, novelties, and regalia of all kinds. Both buildings are typical of substantial late-nineteenth- and early-twentieth-century commercial architecture, with heavy brick bearing walls, wood interior structures, and large street-level display windows.

8-1

8-2

8-2

NORTH MARKET

59 Spruce Street
Circa 1915

AIAC

RENOVATION
1995
Architects: Feinknopf Macioce Schappa, Columbus

Located on the east side of North Front Street between Vine and Spruce streets, the North Market is the city's only remaining enclosed public market. Columbus once had four public markets—Central, East, North, and West. Central was the earliest, built in 1850 on the west side of South Fourth Street between Rich and Town streets. The others followed soon after as the city grew outward. The original North Market was a brick building from the 1880s that burned in the 1940s. In order to keep the market's merchants in business, the city quickly built a new North Market in the form of a large Quonset hut, which was intended as a temporary structure.

"Temporary" can last a long time, and by the late 1980s the old metal hut was well past its prime. By that time, however, with all the other public markets long gone, the City of Columbus realized the value of and the interest in public markets. The high-quality goods offered by the North Market's small independent merchants had really caught on with city (and suburban) residents; as a result, the North Market Development Authority was formed to create a new home for the market.

A former threshing machine factory/warehouse immediately west of the Quonset hut proved the ideal solution. With an interesting interior structure of wood and steel, abundant windows to provide natural light so lacking in the old market, good vertical and horizontal clearances to enable movement of crowds, and a second level for office, restaurant, and dining space, the building underwent a thorough rehabilitation and opened in 1995. The site of the Quonset hut is now the parking lot to the east of the market.

Public markets are lively, noisy, and interesting places to visit. While you are visiting, be sure to sample the freshly made food specialties of the individual merchants, and don't miss the display on the history of the city's public markets on the second floor. An outdoor market is held on Saturdays from early summer to late fall under the new canopy on the east side of the market.

8-3

8-3

ANNUNCIATION GREEK ORTHODOX CATHEDRAL

555 North High Street
1990
Architects: George J. Kontogiannis & Associates, Columbus

Built in traditional Byzantine style in the form of a Greek cross, the Greek Orthodox Cathedral was built as a replacement for the 1922 Hellenic Orthodox Evangelical Church on Park Street. Although the new building replaced several historic commercial buildings, including the long-time favorite Mellman's restaurant, the church has become a welcome neighbor and a real asset for the North Market and Short North districts. It hosts an annual Greek Festival that draws thousands.

The design incorporates traditional Byzantine elements such as arched openings, curved walls, tile roofs, and a large, low dome, as well as a tall bell tower at the southwest corner of the building. The buff brick walls and the tile roof blend well into a cohesive, though complex, design. The church is especially noted for its spectacular interior mosaics. The 1922 church, which received a 1951 addition, remains in use by the church congregation at its original location on Park Street, behind the current church.

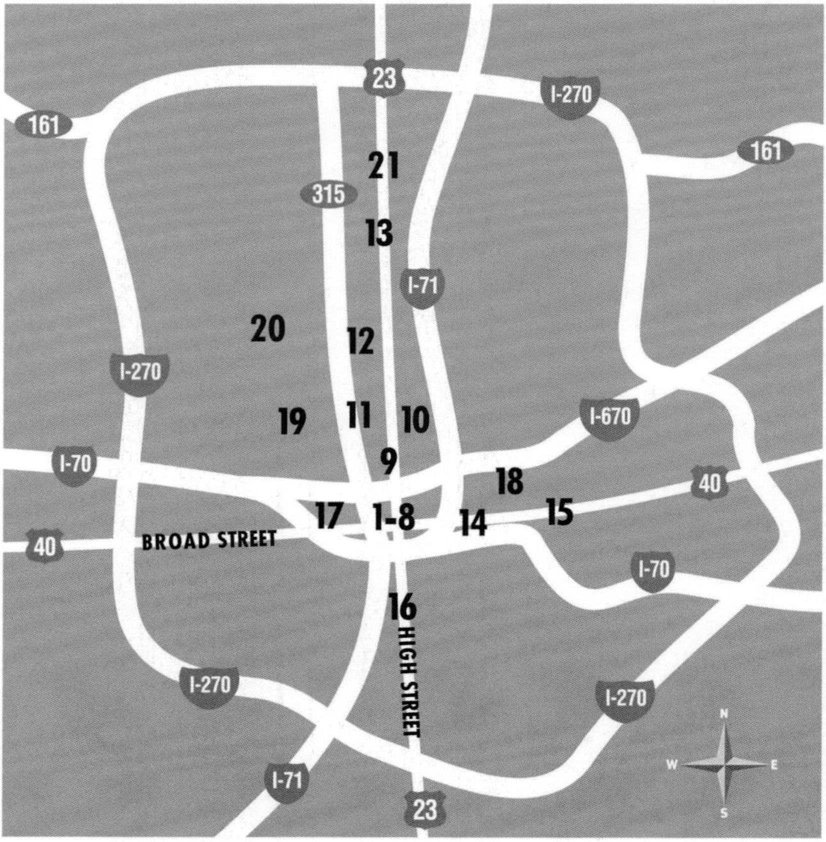

1 CAPITOL SQUARE AREA
2 CIVIC CENTER
3 DOWNTOWN SOUTH HIGH STREET
4 DOWNTOWN EAST SIDE
5 DOWNTOWN EAST BROAD STREET
6 DOWNTOWN NORTH HIGH STREET
7 DOWNTOWN NORTH INNERBELT
8 NORTH MARKET HISTORIC DISTRICT
9 SHORT NORTH HISTORIC DISTRICT
10 ITALIAN VILLAGE HISTORIC DISTRICT
11 VICTORIAN VILLAGE / HARRISON WEST / DENNISON PLACE
12 THE OHIO STATE UNIVERSITY
13 CLINTONVILLE
14 NEAR EAST SIDE
15 BEXLEY
16 GERMAN VILLAGE & HISTORIC DISTRICT
17 FRANKLINTON
18 MOUNT VERNON AREA
19 GRANDVIEW HEIGHTS & MARBLE CLIFF
20 UPPER ARLINGTON
21 WORTHINGTON

Neighborhoods

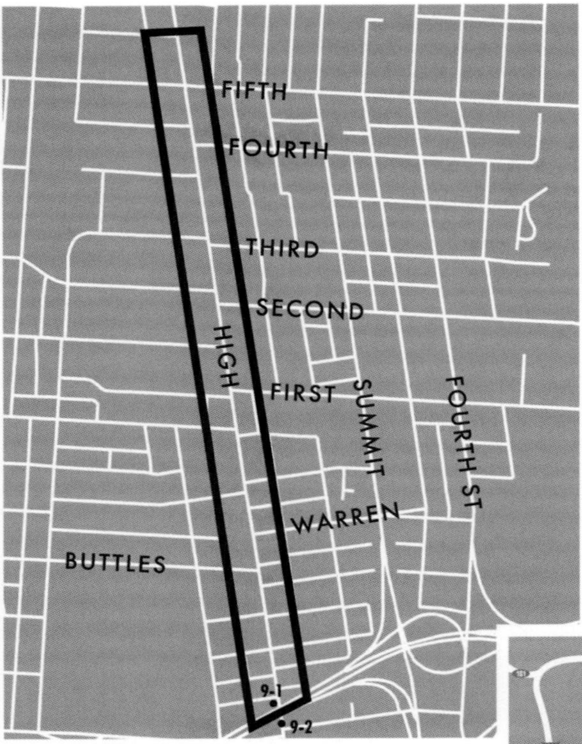

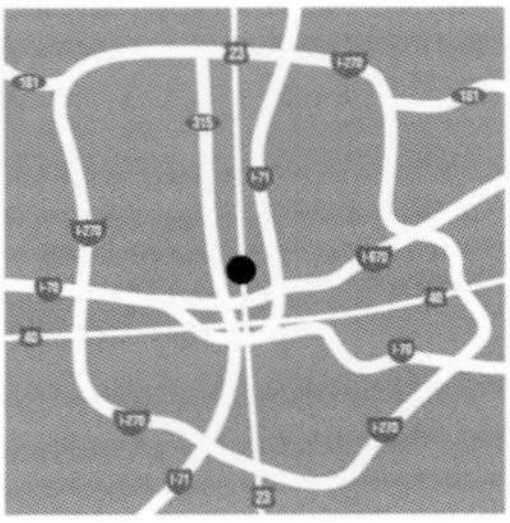

9 SHORT NORTH HISTORIC DISTRICT

9

Short North Historic District

Both sides of North High Street between Poplar Street and Fifth Avenue

Circa 1890–1920

The Short North has become a popular destination in Columbus. Once-empty storefronts on North High Street are now art galleries, restaurants, and shops with apartments and condominiums on upper floors. While North High Street is the center of the Short North, some storefront buildings are on the side streets within a half block of High. The most pleasant way to enjoy the excitement of the Short North is to participate in the Gallery Hop, a giant open house held on the first Saturday evening of each month.

Most structures are of vernacular design; that is, they do not represent any particular style. Brick walls and stone trim predominate; occasionally pressed sheet metal was also used for trim. When High Street was widened in 1915, the facades of the earlier buildings were moved back several feet. Buildings tend to share common features such as height, massing, and setback; the continuous street facades give the district a feeling of compactness and cohesiveness.

Decorative arches, inspired by historic photos of arches in downtown Columbus in the early years of the twentieth century, have been installed over High Street, reinforcing the district's sense of place. Pocket parks with public art and wall murals also enhance the arts-oriented atmosphere of the district.

9-1

9-1
NR, CLF

YUKON BUILDING

601 North High Street
1888; 1929
Italianate

One of the more notable buildings in the area, the Yukon Building anchors the south end of the district. This three-story Italianate building has seven storefronts, label lintels at the windows, and a triangular pediment and nameplate. On the interior, the intervening walls have been removed to create a single first-floor space. The building is being converted into residential condominiums with first-floor retail space.

9-2

9-2
CLF

I-670 CAP

North High Street at the I-670 Innerbelt Freeway
2005
Architects: Meleca Architecture, Columbus

The north leg of the city's Innerbelt freeway had for decades separated the area around Union Station and the North Market from the stretch of North High Street known as the Short North. The conventional freeway bridge over the multilane highway was a major deterrent to pedestrian traffic. With the replacement of Union Station by the Greater Columbus Convention Center and the rebirth of the North Market in a renovated industrial building, along with major investment in the Short North as the city's arts district beginning in the 1980s, pedestrian traffic in the area increased tremendously. It became increasingly apparent that the streetscape gap caused by the old-fashioned freeway bridge had to be closed.

The opportunity for change came in the late 1990s, when reconstruction of the freeway began. Local advocates and the City of Columbus prevailed upon the Ohio Department of Transportation to build the new bridge on High Street as a cap over the freeway on which buildings could be constructed.

Local developer Continental Real Estate Company chose the demolished 1890s Union Station Arcade, which had stood at the crest of the High Street viaduct just to the south, as the design inspiration for the commercial structures lining the freeway cap. To a passing pedestrian, it is not at all apparent that the entire assemblage is a bridge. The storefronts and restaurant spaces have filled up one by one, and today visitors can sit, eat, and shop oblivious to freeway traffic rushing by directly below. This cap is a perfect example of how the scars caused by the construction of urban freeways decades ago can be transformed into lively, pedestrian-oriented places that reconnect the urban fabric.

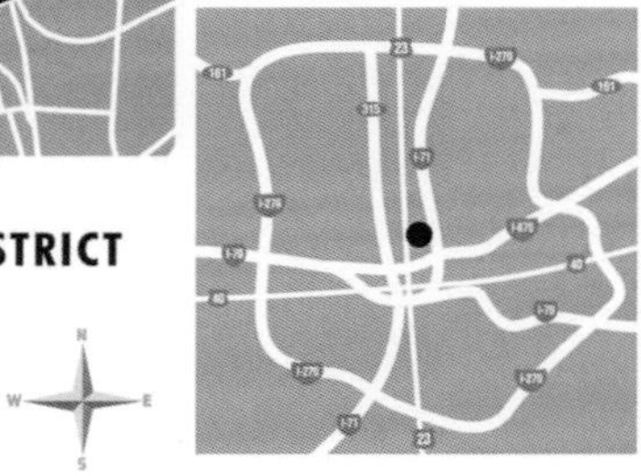

10 ITALIAN VILLAGE HISTORIC DISTRICT

10

Italian Village Historic District

Bounded by North High Street, the CSX Tracks, East Fifth Avenue, and I-670

Home to St. John the Baptist Italian Catholic Church, where Italian masses are still offered, Italian Village is in the midst of a transformation. Formerly an Italian enclave whose residents were attracted by job opportunities in nearby industrial plants, this was a sound and stable working-class neighborhood.

Village architecture combines single-family homes and multifamily apartment buildings. Generally, buildings are two stories high and modest in both scale and execution; brick construction is more common than frame. Although most structures are vernacular in design, many have Italianate features, and some are true Italianate-style buildings.

Recent developments in the area are enhancing the residential character of the district. Taylor Terrace, a 1960s high-rise public housing project on Summit Street between First and Second avenues, was demolished for the construction of New Village Place, a mixed-income residential community that was designed to reintroduce the urban grid and streetscape to the multiblock area. Another major development, Jeffrey Place, is converting the former site of Jeffrey Manufacturing Company on the east edge of Italian Village into a mixed-use urban neighborhood with condominiums, single-family homes, townhouses, commercial uses, and public spaces.

10-1

10-1
NR, CR

ST. JOHN THE BAPTIST ITALIAN CATHOLIC CHURCH

720 Hamlet Street
1898
Late Gothic Revival

ITALIAN CULTURAL CENTER

1989

St. John the Baptist Church was established to serve the Italian American community and continues to do so to this day. The church is widely known as the sponsor of an annual Italian Festival, which spills out into the surrounding streets, creating a lively street party. The building, with its pointed-arch stained-glass windows and entrance, is Late Gothic Revival in design. It is accented with stone trim.

The Italian Cultural Center was built next door to the church in 1989. Constructed of brick, it respects the scale of the surrounding neighborhood and contains decorative elements that reflect the architecture of the church.

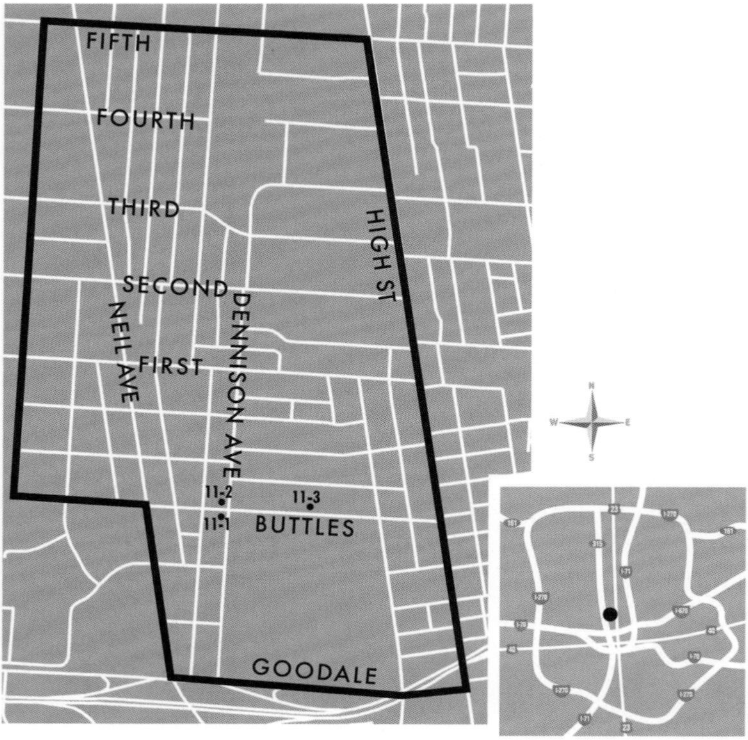

11 VICTORIAN VILLAGE / HARRISON WEST / DENNISON PLACE

11

Victorian Village/ Harrison West/ Dennison Place

Bounded by Goodale Boulevard, Olentangy River, Tenth Avenue, and North High Street

NR, CR

North of downtown and west of the Short North District is a large, pleasant residential area that developed between the 1870s and the 1920s. Listed in the National Register of Historic Places as the Near North Side Historic District, it includes the neighborhoods of Victorian Village, Harrison West, and Dennison Place.

The Near North Side Historic District is primarily residential, with some commercial buildings on major streets and at important intersections and several historic schools and churches scattered throughout. Houses range from very modest frame dwellings to grand mansions. Architectural styles include such late-nineteenth-century styles as Italianate, Queen Anne, and Shingle, as well as early-twentieth-century Colonial Revival and Georgian Revival.

One must-see in this district is Goodale Park at the south end. In 1851 Dr. Lincoln Goodale donated this forty-acre park at 120 Goodale Street to the city, and the park was developed in the 1870s. Near the park's southeast corner, look for the bust of Dr. Goodale, sculpted in 1888 by John Quincy Adams Ward. The substantial stone entrance gates on the south side and northwest corner of the park are also noteworthy, as is the lake in the northeast corner.

West of the park, Neil Avenue runs north from Goodale through the district's heart. It is well worth a stroll. At the turn of the century, industrialists, doctors, and other professionals built most of these large and ornate houses along Neil. Fortunately, very few have been torn down and Neil Avenue remains a residential street. While the buildings are diverse architecturally, they share similar scale, massing, and setback, thus creating a cohesive streetscape.

Harrison West is located west of Harrison Avenue and south of Fifth Avenue. This area of the Near North Side tends to have more modest dwellings, many constructed in frame and more vernacular in character.

The Dennison Park Addition, west of Neil between Fifth and King, was platted in 1888. Anne Dennison originally designed six circular islands at street intersections. Four sixty-foot islands survive, giving the area a sedate and park-like feel. The large brick residences were built between 1888 and 1895.

The many tree-lined streets in the area are worth a close look.

11-1

11-1

PETER SELLS HOUSE

755 Dennison Avenue
1895
Architects: Yost & Packard, Columbus

Peter Sells built this remarkable house, eclectic in design with distinct High Victorian Gothic elements, at the northwest corner of Goodale Park. Dominated by its bellcast pyramidal roof of red tile, the building has warm red brick walls with elaborate detailing. The 8,000-square-foot house features pointed-arch windows and a large, boxy porch, as well as a buttressed porte cochere of generous proportions. A matching carriage house is located at the rear. Inside, the woodwork is carved to display stars and circus motifs.

In the late nineteenth century Peter Sells and his three brothers ran one of the nation's largest circuses, the Sells Brothers Circus. Sellsville, the winter home for the circus, was located not far to the west, on the other side of the Olentangy River. The brothers sold their enterprise to Barnum & Bailey in 1904.

11-2

11-3

11-2

WILLIAM FISH HOUSE

773 Dennison Avenue
Circa 1890

Across the street from the Sells House, the Fish House is vernacular in design, with strong Queen Anne influences. Built by the owner of a stone company, it proved to be a good advertisement for his wares. It features a side entrance porch two stories high, with openwork stone railings. The highly textured rock-faced exterior has smooth-cut stone lintels and sills. Note the decorative gables with a circular tower peeking out of a roof valley.

11-3

BUTTLES AVENUE STREETSCAPE

Buttles Avenue between Park Street and Dennison Avenue

Buttles Avenue, part of the Near North Side Historic District, defines the north edge of the venerable Goodale Park. Significant investment has been occurring in the Near North for over thirty years, and redevelopment of the Short North District, just to the east, has gone on for nearly as long. With its desirable location on the park and its stock of well-preserved historic homes, Buttles Avenue has been a natural draw for new residential development. Some has taken place as renovation of older structures, but availability of vacant sites has spurred some interesting new designs as well.

Long the home of many large and distinguished single-family residences, Buttles Avenue also has some new single-family and multifamily structures that have been carefully designed to fit into the historic streetscape. Some of these are condominium projects built in traditional forms such as rowhouses and carriage houses, and the visitor must look twice to be sure that they are indeed new structures.

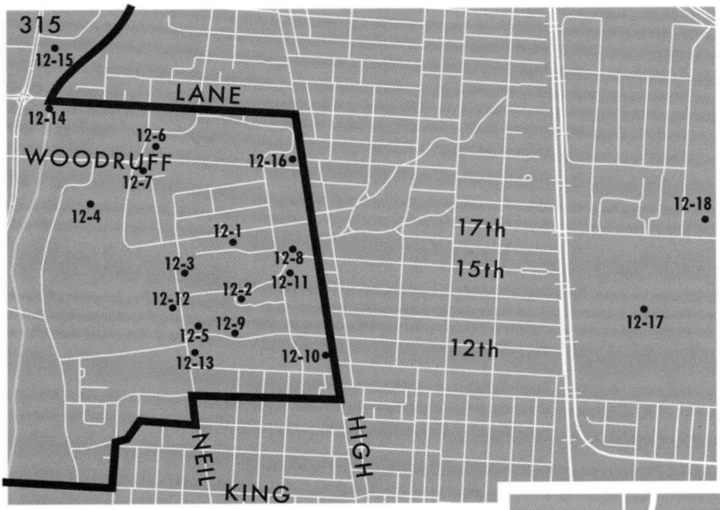

12 THE OHIO STATE UNIVERSITY

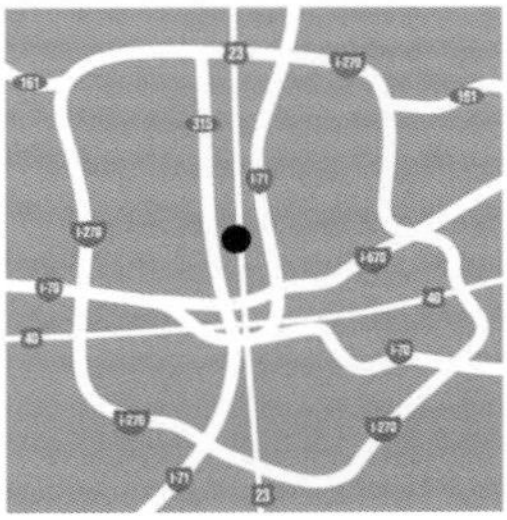

12

The Ohio State University

Established as a land grant college in 1870, the Ohio State University has always been a major Columbus institution and one of the nation's important universities. The university's focal point is the Oval, a large grassy area crisscrossed by pedestrian paths and surrounded by a diverse collection of academic buildings. The university's most historic and architecturally significant buildings are here, too. For example, Hayes and Orton halls date from 1893 and were designed by Columbus architects Yost & Packard, while the Main Library, completed in 1913 with an addition and tower added in 1951, provides a terminus at the west end of the Oval.

The university offers tours of the campus. If you would like to explore the campus on your own, however, be sure to look for these buildings.

12-1

12-2

12-1
NR

HAYES HALL

108 North Oval Drive
1893
Architects: Yost & Packard, Columbus
Romanesque Revival

Hayes Hall is named for former governor and president Rutherford B. Hayes. Its design was based on that of the Harvard Law School. Built of brown sandstone and red pressed brick, the building has the solid, heavy feeling of the Romanesque Revival style. Its main feature is the large entrance arch, which is set into a first floor of rock-faced sandstone. Two-story wings flank the hall's main three-story block.

12-2
NR

ORTON HALL

155 South Oval Drive
1893
Architects: Yost & Packard, Columbus
Richardsonian Romanesque

Across the Oval from Hayes Hall, Orton Hall, named for Edward Orton, OSU's first president, exemplifies the Richardsonian Romanesque style. The style, derived from Romanesque Revival, is named for the architect H. H. Richardson, who made it his own after his successful design of Trinity Church in Boston in the 1880s. Orton Hall features a round tower with a conical roof; within the tower are the well-known OSU chimes. Perhaps because it has always housed the geology department, the hall is built entirely of Ohio stone: forty different varieties, arranged in stratigraphic order as they are found in nature. Details and trim are geology-inspired and represent fossils and extinct animals, like the gargoyles around the top of the tower and at the tops of the columns. The interior of the building is also significant, and the library deserves special mention.

12-3

12-3

WILLIAM OXLEY THOMPSON MEMORIAL LIBRARY

1858 Neil Avenue
1913
Architects: Allen & Collins, Boston
Second Renaissance Revival

ADDITION
1951
Architect: Howard Dwight Smith, OSU

Crowning the west end of the Oval is this Bedford limestone building, named for former OSU president William Oxley Thompson. The building was expanded in 1951 to accommodate a growing university, but the powerful east elevation features the original three-story building. Eight engaged Ionic columns across the front denote the original double-height reading room. Round-arched entrances are set into the rusticated first floor. The addition includes the tower that has become a visual landmark on the Oval.

The building is undergoing a major renovation that will result in the removal of the 1977 addition and construction of a new west wing, the restoration of the two-story height of the historic reading room, and the updating of the tower to include a new penthouse space on the top floor. The renovation, designed by Acock Associates Architects of Columbus and Graham Gund Architects from Boston, is expected to be completed by 2010.

12-4

12-4
NR

OHIO STADIUM

404 West Seventeenth Avenue
1922
Architect: Howard Dwight Smith, OSU

EXPANSION AND RENOVATION
2000
Architects: DesignGroup, Columbus; Hellmuth Obata + Kassabaum, St. Louis

Perhaps no other part of the OSU campus is as close to the hearts of alumni as the famous horseshoe of Ohio Stadium. At the time of its construction, this stadium was the largest west of the Appalachian Mountains. It was also the largest structure of its kind built of reinforced concrete. The innovative double-deck horseshoe is 725 feet long, 596 feet wide, and 98 feet high and measures a third of a mile around its perimeter. It covers ten acres, could originally seat 66,210, and today can seat 101,568.

The stadium was expanded and renovated in 2000. The extensive project included lowering the playing field, creating new locker rooms and band practice rooms, increasing seating capacity, creating a permanent addition at the south end of the stadium, and improving support facilities throughout. The main entrance arch at the north end and the towers at the south end of the stadium were retained as prominent features in the new design. Note the coffered ceiling in the recessed north entrance and the terra-cotta swags between the upper and lower levels.

12-5

12-5

POMERENE HALL

1760 Neil Avenue
1922
Architect: Joseph N. Bradford, OSU
Jacobethan Revival

Pomerene Hall is an excellent example of the Jacobethan Revival style, which is based on elements of English architecture from the sixteenth and seventeenth centuries and was extremely popular for collegiate architecture in the early twentieth century. Asymmetrical in composition but visually unified by its broad slate roof, the building has a square, squat tower within which the main entrance is recessed. Above the arched doorway is a projecting bay of cut stone, with small-paned windows. Similar windows throughout the building are clustered in groups of two to six and framed by cut stone lintels, sills, and trim.

The interior of the building is noteworthy, especially the original dining facility on the ground floor, which still retains its historic pub-like character. The building commands a prime location overlooking Mirror Lake.

12-6
Fisher College of Business
2100 Neil Avenue

MAX M. FISHER HALL

1998
Architects: Cooper Robertson & Partners, New York City; Kallmann McKinnell & Wood, Boston

JOHN B. GERLACH GRADUATE PROGRAMS BUILDING

1998
Architects: Cooper Robertson & Partners, New York City; Kallmann McKinnell & Wood, Boston

SCHOENBAUM UNDERGRADUATE PROGRAM BUILDING

1999
Architects: Karlsberger Companies, Columbus

RAYMOND E. MASON HALL

1999
Architects: Cooper Robertson & Partners, New York City; Kallmann McKinnell & Wood, Boston

JOHN K. PFAHL EXECUTIVE EDUCATION BUILDING

2000
Architects: Cooper Robertson & Partners, New York City; Kallmann McKinnell & Wood, Boston

BLACKWELL INN AT FISHER COLLEGE

2002
Architects: Karlsberger Companies, Columbus

The Fisher College of Business forms a campus-within-a-campus at OSU. Its six buildings form two intersecting quadrangles, and the buildings' shared design characteristics unite them as a single composition. Fisher Hall, the tallest and

12-6

most visible of the six, forms the complex's focal point at the north end of the Huntington Plaza.

All of the buildings have brick exteriors and the traditional rectangular form of early 20th-century academic architecture. Regular window patterns in traditional proportions further reinforce this effect, while rustication of the masonry at corners and on lower floors gives the buildings an additional shared vocabulary. Another contemporary interpretation of past design practice is the slightly projecting brick courses on the upper walls of several of the buildings, a reflection of the projecting cornice that would typically have been found on historic structures.

A contemporary version of a projecting cornice and supporting brackets can be found on Fisher Hall, a feature that distinguishes it from the rest of the complex and reinforces its position as the focal point.

12-7

12-7
AIAC, AIAO

KNOWLTON HALL

275 West Woodruff Avenue
2004
Architects: Mack Scogin Merrill Elam Architects, Atlanta; Wandel & Schnell Architects, Columbus
Landscape Architects: Michael Van Valkenburgh Associates

OSU's Austin E. Knowlton School of Architecture has settled into its new home. In keeping with its function, the building makes a strong architectural statement. Its most distinctive characteristic is the contrast between its exterior surface of white-and-gray marble shingles held in place by special stainless-steel clips and its spatially complex, largely concrete interior. This material makes the building look boxy and firm at some times and fluid and sinuous at others. The whole design defies easy classification—one can argue that it reflects ship design but also that it commemorates nineteenth-century Shingle-style homes, or even contemporary warehouse design.

The building incorporates, in addition to the marble skin, abundant amounts of concrete and glass, all assembled in ways that do not repeat anywhere in the composition. In some areas slender concrete columns make the building seem to hover above its site, while in other places it rests firmly on a solid concrete base. Needless to say, the contrast with the conservative, historically inspired Fisher College of Business just to the north is quite dramatic. The building is a model for the students, providing multiple spatial and circulation types. One of the best interior spaces is the library on the top floor, which is light and airy and sheathed in glass, facing a roof garden not visible from the street.

Along the Knowlton's west elevation is a deep cleft, which is all glass-lined and serves the important function of a light court. It also shelters a collection of historical columns representing all the classical architectural orders. They rest in this narrow slot, ready to be revealed with little warning to the passerby, and remind us that, as different as Knowlton Hall may be from what we have seen before, all design rests upon what came to us from the past.

12-8

12-8
AIA, AIAO, AIAC

WEXNER CENTER FOR THE VISUAL ARTS

30 West Fifteenth Avenue
1989
Architects: Richard Trott & Partners, Columbus; Eisenman Robertson, New York City

RENOVATION
2005
Engineers: Arup Associates, New York City
Architect: OSU University Architect

North of Sullivant Hall and behind Mershon Auditorium is OSU's most daring building, the result of an international design competition. In addition to linking Mershon and Weigel Hall, the Wexner Center provides gallery and performance spaces not available in the other two buildings.

The Wexner Center is skewed off true north by 12 1/4 degrees to reflect the variation of the city and campus street grids. The building is organized around multiples of 12, 24, 48, and 96 to establish the proportional relationship among the various elements. At the south end is a stylized miniature rendition of the old OSU Armory with its crenellated tower; the armory stood on this site until it burned in 1958. From the south end, a modular structural grid rises to the north, its stark vertical and horizontal lines seeming both to float above and to contain the enclosed space below and around it. A permanent sculpture, *Groundswell,* was installed by artist Maya Lin.

12-9

12-9
NR

ENARSON HALL (STUDENT SERVICES BUILDING, OLD OHIO UNION)

154 West Twelfth Avenue
1911
Architect: George S. Mills, Toledo
Jacobethan Revival

RENOVATION
1985
Architects: Coke Harpham, Columbus

Named for past OSU president Harold Enarson, this building was built as the Ohio Union, the first student union to be built on a public university campus and the fourth in the United States. The result of a student-led campaign to establish a social center safe from the vices of the surrounding city, the structure would serve numerous purposes over the years.

Known for its ornamental interior woodwork, the old union building was built in the Jacobethan Revival style, which was very popular on early-twentieth-century college campuses. The style harks back to the ivy-covered walls of staid, traditional English university architecture. Escaping plans for demolition, the building was renovated in 1985. Its exterior design and its important interior architectural features were carefully preserved, and a compatible west wing was constructed to expand usable square footage. Today Enarson Hall houses the offices for undergraduate admissions and the honors and scholarship programs.

12-10

12-10

DRINKO HALL (MICHAEL E. MORITZ COLLEGE OF LAW)

55 West Twelfth Avenue
1958

ADDITION
1993
Architects: Gunnar Birkerts, Birmingham, Michigan; NBBJ, Columbus

Viewed from North High Street, Drinko Hall looks much as it has since its construction: an unassuming, functional building engaged in the serious business of education in the law.

A trip behind the building, however, changes everything. While no taller than the original structure, the 1993 addition is anything but staid and conventional. Composed of two long converging walls that meet at a point oriented to the northwest, the addition seems to speak an entirely different language than the original structure. Windows are punched seemingly at random in the flat masonry walls, and the walls have both projecting and recessed planes and wide rusticated masonry bands. A public entrance on the north elevation near the northwestern tip is framed by paired columns, perhaps an echo of judicial and courthouse architecture of the past. The composition terminates at the tip with a narrow glass trapezoidal form that seems to be striving to reach beyond the confines of the building.

12-11

12-11

JOHN GLENN SCHOOL OF PUBLIC AFFAIRS (PAGE HALL)

1810 College Road
1903
Second Renaissance Revival

RENOVATION
2004
Architects: Lincoln Street Studio, Columbus

Built to house the College of Law and later home to the College of Business, Page Hall was a classically inspired building with strong Renaissance Revival features such as a rusticated raised foundation, pilasters and classical columns, a red tile roof, and a symmetrical composition. While not one of the major landmarks of the OSU campus, Page served long and well, and it was an important component in the assemblage of educational architecture around the Oval.

When the time came to rehabilitate Page Hall, the architect departed significantly from standard rehabilitation practice. From a distance, the completed building still holds its place on the Oval and still has its Second Renaissance Revival features. Up close, however, one can see that much has changed: the former main stairway no longer leads to the entrance, but only to an off-center exit door; the solid brick facade that once stood behind the columns is gone, replaced by shimmering glass; and the main entrance is tucked away in a recess at basement level. On the rear elevation, a tilted glass cube juts beyond the wall plane. The interior is entirely new, only a portion of the exterior walls having been kept during the rehabilitation (the red tile roof is new, too, but is much like the original). Only echoes of the old Page are left, but the new Page, home of the John Glenn School of Public Affairs, blends with the old to make a bold statement.

As a contrast in design approach, have a look at Hagerty Hall just to the west of Page.

12-12

12-12
Campbell, Lazenby, Townshend Hall Group

CAMPBELL HALL

1787 Neil Avenue
1916
Architect: Joseph N. Bradford, OSU
Neoclassical Revival

LAZENBY HALL

1827 Neil Avenue
1915
Architect: Joseph N. Bradford, OSU
Second Renaissance Revival

TOWNSHEND HALL

1885 Neil Avenue
1898
Architects: Peters, Burns & Pretzinger, Dayton
Second Renaissance Revival

Campbell, Lazenby, and Townshend halls form a triumvirate of traditional academic architecture from the late nineteenth and early twentieth centuries. Built in a row along the west side of Neil Avenue, they anchor the west edge of the Oval and the oldest part of the Ohio State campus. They share several design elements, including a symmetrical plan, a central pavilion with flanking pavilions linked by recessed wings, ornate triple-arched central entrances, and walls of brick and stone.

Campbell is Neoclassical Revival in style, while Lazenby and Townshend have all the hallmarks of the Second Renaissance Revival style. All three, however, share classically inspired stylistic elements common to both styles, including the rusticated raised basement and first floor, more plainly detailed upper floors, and a distinct termination of the upper wall at the roof. Campbell's terminating element is a projecting cornice, while Lazenby and Townshend have projecting roof eaves with exposed rafters, a common feature of Second Renaissance Revival–style buildings.

All three buildings have received renovations and additions over the years and remain in excellent condition and in full use for academic purposes.

12-13
Oxley, Mack Hall Group

OXLEY HALL

1712 Neil Avenue

1910

Architects: Florence Kenyon Hayden, Columbus; Wilbur T. Mills, Columbus

MACK HALL

1694 Neil Avenue

1923

Architect: Joseph N. Bradford, OSU

Jacobethan Revival

ADDITION

1934

Architect: Howard Dwight Smith, OSU

RENOVATION

2000

Architects: Schooley Caldwell Associates, Columbus

Oxley and Mack halls sit side by side in the long row of academic buildings that line Neil Avenue on the OSU campus. Built less than fifteen years apart, they exemplify the early-twentieth-century evolution of academic building design.

Oxley Hall is the only major historic building in Columbus known to have been designed by a woman. Kenyon Hayden (the name by which she was best known) did residential work in the city and appears to have been chosen personally by University Architect Joseph Bradford for the Oxley project; Wilbur Mills served as advisory architect on the project. Oxley was the first women's dormitory on the OSU campus.

Oxley Hall is a substantial red brick structure that does not represent any particular style. However, its corner tower and crenellations are an early suggestion of the Collegiate Gothic and Jacobethan Revival designs that soon would become the norm for academic buildings on campuses across the country.

Mack Hall, by comparison, is a fully developed example of Jacobethan Revival design. Here one can find the oriel window, the half-timbering, the ornate brickwork and detailed carved stone, the wall buttresses, and the small-paned casement windows characteristic of the style. The sign in front of Mack Hall describes it as the "Stadium Scholarship Dormitory." The reason is that the renovation and expansion of Ohio Stadium in the late 1990s required that the

12-13

scholarship dorm that had been located under the west side of the stadium since 1933 be permanently removed. To make the transition less traumatic for the dorm's occupants, the university decided to renovate a single building to keep the students together. The size and high quality of Mack Hall made it the ideal candidate.

12-14

12-14

LANE AVENUE BRIDGE

West Lane Avenue at Olentangy River
2003
Engineers: Dean C. Ringle, Franklin County Engineer; Jones-Stuckey Ltd., Columbus

One of the most distinctive bridges in the Columbus area, the Lane Avenue Bridge is an example of a cable-stayed suspension design. In contrast to traditional suspension bridges (such as the Golden Gate or the Brooklyn Bridge), cable-stayed structures use multiple rather than paired cables to support and stabilize the roadway. The 370-foot span over the Olentangy River employs 10,000 cubic yards of concrete and 500 tons of structural steel; the twin support towers rise 165 feet above the water, and the total length of the strands in the polyethylene-sheathed cables is 8.5 miles.

The design incorporates generous sidewalks and large plazas at either end. The rustication on the towers, the center pier, and along the wingwalls of the abutments adds a sense of refinement, while stairs to the riverbank provide access to walkways along the water.

12-15

12-15
AIAC

LONGABERGER ALUMNI HOUSE

2200 Olentangy River Road
1999
Architects: Wandel & Schnell, Columbus

Located just south of OSU's venerable Fawcett Center and sited between the Olentangy River and Olentangy River Road, the Longaberger Alumni House was built entirely with private support from all parts of Ohio and the nation. Major support came from the Longaberger Foundation, which was established by the Longaberger Basket Company of Muskingum County, Ohio.

Alumni groups on the OSU campus had long been short on space, and a single location for all of them seemed the right answer. The facility includes conference, gallery, and dining space and can host multiple events at once. It is available for private events not associated with university activities, of which it hosts more than a thousand a year.

The building's main elevation faces north, where the recessed entry is set behind a row of concrete columns; the same recess shelters a wheelchair ramp. Further shelter is provided by a cable-suspended metal canopy that runs the length of the main elevation and terminates in a modest porte cochere at the east end of the building. Vertical banks of windows provide generous interior light.

The Longaberger Alumni House is connected by pathways to the Richard and Annette Bloch Cancer Survivors Plaza, which is located next to the river and is connected by walkway to the Lane Avenue Bridge. By means of the bridge, a visitor may walk to any part of the OSU campus.

Surrounding Area

The presence of the university has greatly influenced the area around it. To the east of High Street is a large residential district with an early-twentieth-century character. It is bounded roughly by Lane Avenue, Fourth Street, and Tenth Avenue. For many years, student housing has concentrated here. Especially in the last ten years, apartment buildings have replaced many older homes due to constant pressures to increase residential density.

A drive or walk around the neighborhood is still worthwhile, however. Here and there you'll see some earlier Queen Anne and late Victorian structures. Later houses, apartment buildings, and fraternity and sorority houses represent just about every twentieth-century residential style.

South of the OSU campus are the northern fringes of the Victorian Village residential district, whose axis is Neil Avenue. The Short North, a historic commercial area that has been transformed into an arts district, extends from downtown to the campus area along High Street. The University Gateway at the south end of campus is a new mixed-use development that is a catalyst for further investment along this section of High Street.

12-16

12-16

ST. STEPHEN'S EPISCOPAL CHURCH

30 West Woodruff

1951

Architects: Brooks & Coddington, Columbus

Although not built on OSU property, St. Stephen's has long been a part of campus life. With its spare, simple design dominated by the steeply pitched gable roof oriented toward the street and its extensive use of glass, it is a classic 1950s modern building. Steel beams that meet at the roof peak support the main church structure, leaving the entire interior open and enabling the use of a full glass wall at the south end. The projecting tile roof forms a sheltered entry held up by plain steel columns. These continue to the west as supports for a flat roof over a walkway to other church facilities. The side and end walls are of brick, and wings and additions use the same wall and roof materials.

Noteworthy features include the interior, which is flooded with natural light, and the glass wall overlooking the screened landscaped courtyard space.

12-17a

12-17b

12-17c

12-17

OHIO STATE EXPOSITION CENTER

Bounded by Norfolk Southern Railroad, I-71, Seventeenth Avenue, and Eleventh Avenue
1886

In October of 1850 Camp Washington, near Cincinnati, hosted the first Ohio State Fair. After moving around the state, the fair came to Columbus in 1874 and stayed. Franklin Park on East Broad Street was the State Fairgrounds until 1886, when the fair moved to its current 150-acre site. The country's second oldest fair, and one of the largest, it takes place in early August.

The oldest building on the fairgrounds is near the Eleventh Avenue entrance, the 1888 South Commercial Exhibits Building, and between two similar buildings dating from 1905. All three have large timber-framed structures with open sides and broad roofs. Note that they feature the Queen Anne–style decorative treatment typical of their era, evident in their lively wall surfaces, towers, and decorative woodwork.

Other early buildings include the brick Administrative Building, built before 1911; the brick Women's Building, dating from 1909; and the brick Boys' and Girls' and Dairy Buildings. The Coliseum, completed in 1917, is still used for circuses, horse shows, and other events. Enlarged in 1991, it is one of the largest structures on the fairground.

Near the northwest corner of the Fairgrounds is the Gilligan Livestock Complex, built in the late 1970s. This reinforced-concrete building has a parking garage on its upper level. In 1991 the 12,000-seat Celeste Building replaced an outdoor grandstand as a concert site. The Eleventh Avenue entrance is marked by the large OHIO structure, which replaced an earlier ticket booth and gate spelling out "OHIO" in big red letters.

12-18

12-18
AIAO

OHIO HISTORICAL CENTER

1982 Velma Avenue (I-71 at 17th Avenue)
1970
Architects: W. Byron Ireland & Associates, Columbus
Brutalist

The Ohio Historical Society created quite a stir when it constructed this building on the north end of the Ohio State Fairgrounds. The Brutalist design of this memorable building is one not typically associated with a historical organization. Its monumental scale, daring structural design using post-tensioned concrete, and simple forms received considerable attention in the architectural and general press.

The center sits on what appears to be a mounded site. In reality, however, the museum and office space under the sloping lawns to the north and south are at ground level. At the next level is the main entrance in a glassed-in plaza. High above, the large, brown, boxy structure, finished in Ohio silo tile, seems to float over the site. The design is deceptive, as this portion of the building houses a large library reading room with skylights in the center with offices around the perimeter. The space also includes archival space and two floors of library stacks.

North of the main building is Ohio Village, a collection of buildings constructed in the mid-1970s. Based on numerous Ohio architectural models, the Village depicts a typical small Ohio community in about 1850.

13 Clintonville

Bounded by the Olentangy River, Henderson and Cooke Roads, Indianola Avenue, and Arcadia Avenue

Named after Clinton Township, Clintonville is primarily a residential area developed from the 1920s through the 1940s. Houses are generally small in scale, on small lots, of frame construction, and well preserved. The area features uniform setbacks from street to street, abundant trees, and, in some areas, historic streetlights. A particularly attractive area of Clintonville to visit lies north of Oakland Park Avenue and south of Glenmont Avenue, east of High Street.

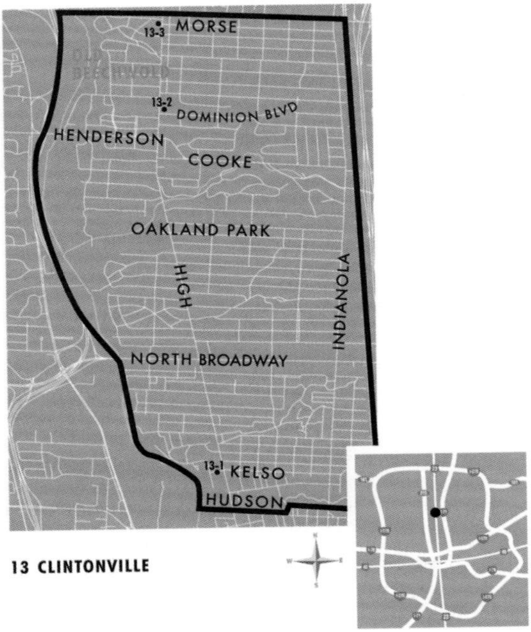

13 CLINTONVILLE

13-1

13-1

OLENTANGY VILLAGE

2800 North High Street
1939
Architect: Raymond P. Snow, Washington, DC
Georgian Colonial Revival

Built on the former site of Olentangy Park, an amusement park developed by the Columbus Street Railway Company, Olentangy Village is a 402-unit apartment complex. Developer L. L. LeVeque chose Raymond P. Snow, an architect well known for designing garden apartments and for using Georgian Colonial Revival style.

LeVeque wanted to preserve the large trees and natural beauty of the site. Despite its size, the complex lacks a crowded or dense feeling. To create an atmosphere of graciousness and space, Snow limited building heights to two or three stories. He also broke up wall surfaces by using irregular plans to create a series of apartment clusters on courtyards. To isolate the complex, he placed all buildings well back from High Street. Commercial buildings on either side of the village's entrance form a gateway and separate the complex from the street.

In the late 1980s two new apartment developments were added to the sixty-one-acre site, the River and the Ravine, as well as the Cove and Point condominiums.

13-2

13-2

OUR LADY OF PEACE CHURCH

20 East Dominion
1966
Architect: Ernest Gaal, Columbus

The church's powerful design includes a low-pitched pyramidal roof and strong battered-brick corner columns. Its main feature is a stylized metal steeple. Though it suggests a traditional steeple that might be found on an older church, only the essential structure has been built, leaving the church bells exposed.

The interior of the church is also interesting. It was influenced by the architecture of Eero Saarinen, one of the most innovative architects practicing in the early to mid-twentieth century.

Old Beechwold Historic District

13-3

NR, CR

Bounded by West Jeffrey Place, North High Street, Rustic Place/Riverview Park Drive, and the Olentangy River

Originally developed as a zoo, which occupied this site until 1902, the location was ideal for residential development; it was eight miles from downtown Columbus and well outside the city limits. After the zoo failed, a local manufacturer of mining equipment, Joseph A. Jeffrey, bought these seventy-five wooded acres in 1906. The same year Jeffrey built an English cottage on his new private estate, which he named Beechwalde, meaning "beech forest."

Joseph A. Jeffrey's home still stands at 150 West Beechwold Boulevard. His English cottage has rubble stone walls and Renaissance Revival detailing in its round-arched openings and column-enclosed, recessed entrance.

Columbus developer Charles H. Johnson bought Jeffrey's property in 1914. According to a 1981 *Columbus Dispatch* article, it was Johnson who changed the spelling from

13-3

"Beechwalde" to "Beechwold." Beechwold became one of the ninety-nine subdivisions in and around the city that Johnson eventually developed. The Beechwold Realty Company platted the land in 1915 according to a plan by landscape architect William Pitkin, Jr., of Cleveland. Over the next twenty-five years the company built some 150 houses for upper-middle-class business and professional people. Two events helped to ensure the success of the development: the widening of North High Street and the extension of street railway lines to the area.

As was the mode at the time, builders used mainly picturesque revival designs:

ENGLISH COTTAGE: Rubble stone walls, steep gabled roofs, half-timbered walls.

TUDOR REVIVAL: Steeply pitched roofs, half-timbered or stucco walls, projecting arched entrances, tall chimneys.

GEORGIAN REVIVAL: Gabled roof; often dormers have classical details, porticoes (columned porches), corner quoins, belt courses (horizontal bands), Flemish bond brickwork (ends of bricks alternate with sides).

DUTCH COLONIAL REVIVAL: Gambrel roofs with different pitches on each side, dormers the full length of the house, multipaned upper sashes, lunette (half-moon) windows in gable ends.

SPANISH COLONIAL REVIVAL: Tile roofs, adobe or stucco walls, iron window grilles, balconies.

CRAFTSMAN: Low-pitched overhanging roofs with projecting eaves, multipaned upper sashes, false roof beams in gable ends, battered posts on full-length porches.

14

Near East Side

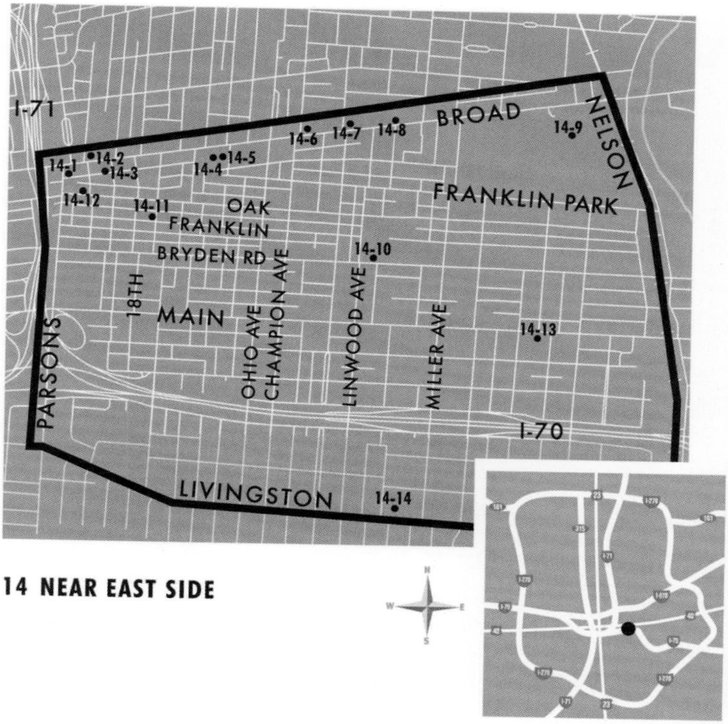

14 NEAR EAST SIDE

East Broad Street

Bounded by I-71 and Nelson Road

NR

From the city's earliest days, East Broad Street has been the showcase street, the most desired address, the location of many of the city's largest mansions. Originally Broad extended eastward only to Fourth Street. It was extended to Parsons Avenue in 1842, to Twentieth Street in 1863, to Alum Creek by 1870, and beyond by 1891. At the turn of the twentieth century, Broad Street was distinguished by twin landscaped parkways that extended all the way to the heart of the downtown area.

The wealthy and powerful of Columbus built their homes on East Broad, and it remained primarily a street of large single-family homes until the early twentieth century, when apartment buildings targeting an affluent market began to appear. Several historic churches and East High School were interspersed among the residential uses. Today the vast majority of buildings along East Broad Street date from the late nineteenth to the early twentieth centuries. These structures have been recognized through listing in the National Register of Historic Places.

The character of East Broad Street has changed over the years. The city removed the twin parkways in the late 1920s to accommodate automobile traffic. Gradually many of the large homes were converted to office uses, and a number have been demolished to be replaced by more modern office buildings, or in some cases parking lots and filling stations. In spite of the changes, East Broad Street remains an attractive tree-lined major thoroughfare.

14-1
NR, CR

W. H. JONES MANSION

731 East Broad Street
Circa 1885
Queen Anne

Named after the successful dry goods merchant who built it, the Jones mansion, with its irregular massing, complex rooflines, variety of window shapes and sizes, and corner turret, is Queen Anne in design. It is built of brick and has trim and details of stone, terra-cotta, wood, and wrought iron. Much of the interior remains intact, including the curved staircase and the third-floor ballroom, a common element of many of the city's finest homes of the period. Behind the house is a large carriage house with room for multiple vehicles, as well as living space above. Its brick-and-wood-shingle exterior, slate roof, and corner turret are all original.

14-2

14-2
NR

BROAD STREET PRESBYTERIAN CHURCH

760 East Broad Street
1894
Architect: Elah Terrell, Columbus
Richardsonian Romanesque

ADDITION
1908
Architect: Frank L. Packard, Columbus

INTERIOR ALTERATIONS
1937
Architects; Richards McCarty & Bulford, Columbus

AIAO, AIAC

ADDITION
1985
Architects: Trott & Bean Architects, Columbus

ADDITION
2005
Architects: Rogers Krajnak Architects, Columbus

Typical of the Richardsonian Romanesque style, Broad Street Presbyterian Church has a heavy, imposing character. Distinguishing features include round-arched openings; limestone exterior with contrasting red sandstone around the windows and doors; corner bell tower with steeple; and stained-glass windows from the famed Tiffany Studios as well as local companies Von Gerichten Art Glass Company and Franklin Art Glass Company.

The church has been expanded several times, creating a large complex of interconnecting structures. A landscaped park area was developed by the church immediately to the east along East Broad Street. The scale of this building and its steeple make it a neighborhood landmark.

14-3

14-4

14-3

ST. PAUL'S EPISCOPAL CHURCH

787 East Broad Street
1903
Architect: Frank L. Packard, Columbus
Late Gothic Revival

St. Paul's was the work of one the city's most accomplished late-nineteenth- and early-twentieth-century architects. Though modest in size and scale, the church features forms and details typical of the huge Gothic cathedrals of Europe. Most prominent is the large traceried window over the main entrance on the north elevation. The design is repeated in smaller arched windows set into the stone walls. The stonework is quite elegant, a restrained and well-executed blend of rock-faced walls and smooth belt courses, parapets, and corner quoins.

On the interior, St. Paul's has long been recognized for its beautiful woodwork. The paneled choir in the apse, the screen in front of the apse, and the massive ornamental beams in the nave are excellent examples of the woodworker's art.

14-4
NR

HANNA HOUSE

1021 East Broad Street
1896

James B. Hanna, the cofounder of one of Ohio's leading paint companies, built this home. Its eclectic design combines elements of Beaux-Arts and Neoclassical Revival styles. The house features a stately columned front porch, paired windows, a projecting second-floor bay window, a broad frieze beneath a bracketed cornice, and an ornate pedimented central dormer set into the red tile roof.

14-5
NR

BROAD STREET CHRISTIAN CHURCH

1049 East Broad Street
1907
Architect: Wilbur T. Mills, Columbus

Broad Street Christian is a substantial stone church with a heavily textured rock-faced surface. Built of blue freestone, its eclectic design includes round-arched openings reminiscent of Richardsonian Romanesque and a square bell tower with a hipped roof and wide overhanging eaves typical of the Arts and Crafts movement. The red tile roof adds color and richness of texture to the building.

14-6

14-6
NR

COLUMBUS FOUNDATION (OLD GOVERNOR'S MANSION)

1234 East Broad Street
1904
Architect: Frank L. Packard, Columbus
Georgian Revival

AIAC
RENOVATION
1987
Architects: Richard Trott and Partners, Columbus

Charles Lindenberg, president of the Lilley Regalia Company, once the world's largest manufacturer of fraternal regalia, built this mansion. Note the building's symmetry and high-contrast exterior of brick and rusticated stone. The dormers in the roof admitted light to the spacious third-floor ballroom. Lindenberg hired Frederick Law Olmsted to design the grounds, which included a sunken garden. Today the landscaped grounds include a garden pergola. The original carriage house remains at the rear of the property.

The state purchased this mansion in 1919 for $75,000 and used it as the governor's mansion until 1957. Following a brief stint as a state archives, it had several owners in the 1970s. The old governor's mansion was rehabilitated in 1987 as the home of the city's principal private foundation, the Columbus Foundation.

14-7a

14-7b

14-7
Broad Street Apartments

Luxury apartment buildings were introduced into the Broad Street area during the 1920s and 1930s. These included three- and four-story buildings arranged around landscaped courtyards such as the Broadmoor Apartments at 880 East Broad and Governor's Terrace at 1160–90 East Broad. High-rise apartments also became popular. Two of the most notable are the Broadwin and Royal York apartment buildings.

THE BROADWIN

NR
1312 East Broad Street
1925
Second Renaissance Revival

The Broadwin is one of several early-twentieth-century apartment buildings that were constructed along Broad Street as it continued to evolve from single-family home to mixed uses. It is an imposing building constructed in a tripartite arrangement typical of the period. The two-story base is clad in rusticated stone, the third through eighth floors are plain brick with stone corner quoins and belt-courses, and a pronounced cornice completes the composition. The gracious central entrance leads to the marble-floored, wood-paneled lobby. The building originally had an elegant restaurant on the first floor, and its location is still visible today at the rear of the lobby.

ROYAL YORK APARTMENTS

NR
1445 East Broad Street
1937
Art Moderne

A park-like setting softens the starkness of this large Art Moderne apartment building. The structure is all geometric shapes and vertical lines; the brick exterior and the windows have little ornamentation. Its eight stories are topped by a penthouse with a wonderful Art Deco interior and spectacular city views.

14-8

14-8
NR

BAKER/TAYLOR RESIDENCE

1400 East Broad Street
1856
Italian Villa

Dr. Baker lived in this brick house for only two years, but members of the Taylor family continued to live in the house until the mid-1990s. One of the oldest surviving buildings on East Broad Street, it would have been well outside the city limits at the time it was constructed. Its segmental-arched windows, cornice brackets, and decorative wood front porch are important features of the Italian Villa style. The site for the house is raised above the level of East Broad Street, which gives the building an imposing character for its relatively modest size.

14-9a

14-9
NR

FRANKLIN PARK CONSERVATORY

1800 East Broad Street
1895
Architect: J. M. Freese, Columbus

AIAC

EXPANSION
1992
Architects: Böhm-NBBJ, Columbus

Franklin Park and the Franklin Park Conservatory are gems in the Columbus park system. Franklin Park is located on what had been the site of the Ohio State Fair from 1874 to 1886, when the fair moved to its current location. In 1895 the city built a conservatory near the northeast corner of the park. This $24,000 building featured an elegant palm house, smaller greenhouses for growing, as well as administrative space. The Palm House features a curved roofline, a central entrance flanked by glass turrets, and a large iron-and-glass lantern in the center of the roofline. The conservatory's ornate entrance on the west side was removed

14-9b

in 1957 and restored in 1991 when the building was expanded and renovated to host Ameriflora, an international flower show, in 1992. The current conservatory is four times as large as the original and features a variety of growing environments as part of its permanent horticultural display. Near the west entrance is Stephen Canneto's thirty-foot-tall sculpture *NavStar;* its stainless steel billowing sails represent Christopher Columbus's three ships. The 110-acre park is surrounded by a residential neighborhood. Among the distinctive features in the park are the lake and cascades with flowing water along the southern edge, the superintendent's cottage, and the 1915 picnic shelter and recreation building.

Near East Side Historic District

Bounded by I-71, Broad Street, Main Street, and Alum Creek
NR

By the mid-nineteenth century Columbus had outgrown its immediate downtown area and had begun to expand to the east. Early on, commercial and residential buildings intermingled within the first few blocks out from Capitol Square, but the streets soon became residential in character. Wealthy, influential people built their homes and churches on Broad Street and Town Street or its eastward extension, Bryden Road.

A large residential area east of Parsons Avenue between Broad and Main Streets developed between the 1880s and 1920s. The area is characterized by single-family homes with uniform setbacks, and brick is the predominant building material. Small landscaped front yards and tree-lined streets create a pleasant backdrop for the wide variety of architectural styles found here. Several churches and schools are interspersed among the homes, but there is little commercial development, with the exception of Parsons Avenue on the western edge of the neighborhood.

Bryden Road is considered the premier street in this district, lined with many of the most impressive homes in the area.

14-10

14-11

14-10
NR, CR

CHARLES FREDERICK MYERS HOUSE

1330 Bryden Road
1896

A German immigrant, C. F. Myers became wealthy through his United States Carriage Works on Fourth Street. His eighteen-room house, an eclectic design with French and German Renaissance influences, is one of the most distinctive in the city. Its most powerful element is the square tower at the southwest corner, built of multicolored brick laid in a diagonal pattern. The features of this visual delight include steep tile roofs, decorative chimneys, terra-cotta ornamentation, ornate dormers, and a wonderfully complex asymmetrical composition. The ornate fence and gate along the sidewalk are recent additions.

14-11
NR

FLORENCE KENYON HAYDEN RECTOR HOUSE

878 Franklin Avenue
1926
Architect: Florence Kenyon Hayden Rector, Columbus

Florence Rector was not only the first woman architect licensed in the state but also the only woman architect practicing in central Ohio between 1900 and 1930. The long, narrow home she designed for herself is a stuccoed two-and-a-half-story structure. With its gable end to the street, the house is modest and has a distinctly asymmetrical front facade. It combines French doors, small rectangular windows, round-headed windows, and steel casements in an eclectic and very personal design.

14-12
NR

COLUMBUS MUSIC HALL (ENGINE HOUSE NO. 12)

734 Oak Street
1900

RENOVATION
1986

Built at the turn of the century, this building, with its brick exterior, large wooden doors for fire equipment, and tower for drying hoses, looked like other fire stations of the period. Before the city's Cultural Arts Center was created in 1978, this building was used for many years as an arts-and-crafts center for the Columbus Recreation and Parks Department. The building retains its original character on the exterior, while the interior spaces have been sensitively modified for its current use as a music hall and entertainment venue.

14-13

ROCK OF FAITH BAPTIST CHURCH (HOLY ROSARY CHURCH)

1651 East Main Street
1915
Architect: Harvey H. Heistand, Columbus

RECTORY

Circa 1845

The 1845 former rectory, the oldest of these buildings, has an interesting history. After the American Revolution, the government set aside a 100,000-acre parcel of land, known as the Refugee Tract, to compensate Canadians who had been driven from their lands for supporting the colonial cause. An early house in the Refugee Tract became today's Holy Rosary rectory. A typical brick house of the time, it has two stories, a gable roof, and a main entrance flanked by sidelights and a transom. The wooden front porch is the former rectory's most decorative feature.

The church itself is reminiscent of medieval Italian rural churches. It features a tall campanile (bell tower) beside the main building, which is in the basilica form originally developed by the ancient Romans. A rounded apse and Romanesque round arches enhance the European feel of the structure, as do the red tile roofs and unusual brick bonding. No special brick shapes were used to create the diamond pattern on the walls; it was achieved solely by varying the ways the bricks were bonded. In the 1980s the Catholic congregation merged with St. John the Evangelist Church on Ohio Avenue and this church was occupied by the current congregation.

14-14

14-14

NHL, NR, CR

EDDIE RICKENBACKER HOUSE

1334 East Livingston Avenue
Circa 1895

This unassuming cottage was the boyhood home of Captain Edward V. Rickenbacker, the nation's most famous World War I flying ace, who also had a distinguished civil aviation career. It is one of only three National Historic Landmarks in Columbus. Rickenbacker's father built the home over a period of several years. When the family moved here, the house was located at the edge of the city. A large garden in the rear provided food for the large financially struggling family. Following his father's untimely death, Rickenbacker left school at a young age and pursued a successful career as a race-car driver. His winnings from racing helped him make improvements to the property. The building is now owned by the City of Columbus, and plans are underway to restore it to its original appearance and adapt it into a museum.

I-670
15-7
15-4
MARYLAND AVE
NELSON RD
15-3
15-8
CLIFTON AVE
BROAD
GOULD RD
15-5
15-2
15-1
PARKVIEW AVE
DREXEL AVE
CASSADY AVE
FAIR AVE
15-6
MAIN ST
I-70
N
W
E
S

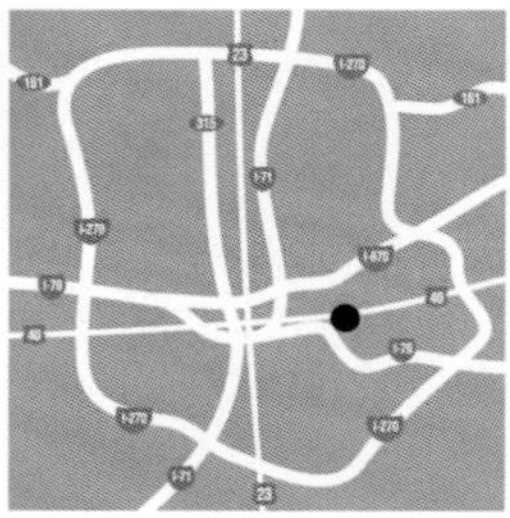

15 BEXLEY

15

Bexley

Bounded by Alum Creek, Delmar Drive, Gould Avenue, and Livingston Avenue

Bexley is one of the city's early automobile suburbs. Located on the east side approximately three miles from downtown, the community has a rich mix of early-twentieth-century architecture in three distinct areas. South Bexley, between Livingston and Main streets, contains modestly scaled early-twentieth-century homes situated on narrow lots with garages located along alleys. Central Bexley, between Main and Broad Streets, has larger homes on larger lots. Several of the streets have landscaped medians. North Bexley has large estate homes on large lots with greater setbacks. Main Street is the commercial center of Bexley, with the city hall, Bexley Public Library, Montrose School, and Capital University interspersed with commercial buildings from all eras. The entire community features tree-lined streets with sidewalks, making it very pedestrian-friendly.

15-1

15-2

15-1

FRANCIS SESSIONS OCTAGON HOUSE

2130 East Broad Street
Circa 1855

A very early house well hidden in tall trees, the Sessions House looks deceptively conventional because of its projecting east and west two-story wings. It truly is, however, an octagon. A brick structure with a stuccoed exterior, it has six-over-six-pane rectangular windows and a pedimented entrance. The interior features a sweeping stairway and fine woodwork around doors, windows, and mantels.

Octagon houses enjoyed a brief period of popularity following the publication in 1849 of *The Octagon House: A Home for All,* by Orson Squire Fowler. Fowler correctly stated that octagons enclose more space within a given wall length than rectangular houses; however, his claim that octagons would cure sexual perversion remains unsubstantiated. Not many Ohioans built octagonal homes; fewer than twenty remain in the state.

15-2
NR

SESSIONS VILLAGE

Sessions Drive off East Broad Street
1926–31
Architects: Miller & Reeves, Columbus
French Provincial

Immediately west of the Sessions House is an elegantly planned community, Sessions Village. After considerable travel in Europe, the architects developed this village design as a careful reproduction of a village in Provence. The original promotional literature described Sessions Village as a place "where the spirit may grow and the pettiness of the work-a-day world be forgotten." The intimate scale, a combination of freestanding and attached buildings located close to the street, small walled gardens and courtyards and careful blending of features like the bridge room over the drive, carved stone details, rubble stone and brick walls, casement windows, half-timbering, and a small public town square with a fountain and stone paving—all of these indeed created an environment that seems far from central Ohio. During the second half of the twentieth century, newer buildings were added to the original ten along Sessions Drive. Unlike the homes in the original development, these homes are all detached single-family homes with front yards.

15-3

15-3

ROBERT JEFFREY MANSION

195 North Parkview
1905
Architect: Frank L. Packard, Columbus
Jacobethan Revival

After working at the Jeffrey Manufacturing Company, the founder's son, Robert Jeffrey, turned to politics and in 1903, at the age of 29, became mayor of Columbus. After three years he returned to the family firm, where he remained for the rest of his career.

Note the mansion's many Jacobethan Revival design features: brick walls with cut stone trim, multiple casement windows, and ornamented doorways. Crenellations on the tops of some walls are reminiscent of English castles. The entrance area dates from 1922, and the south wings, porte cochere, and west terrace from 1926. The elevated west terrace provides expansive views over the property.

In 1941 Jeffrey donated the house to the city of Bexley to be used as a community center. Jeffrey Mansion is located within a park of nearly forty acres. Facilities include a large lawn behind the house, picnic shelter, tennis courts, a community swimming pool, and trails through the woods along Alum Creek.

15-4

15-4

NR

GOVERNOR'S RESIDENCE (JEFFREY HOUSE)

358 North Parkview Avenue

1925

Architect: Robert Gilmore Hanford, Columbus

Jacobethan Revival

The Malcolm Jeffrey House was donated to the State of Ohio by the Reverend Charles and Janet Harris in 1957 and became the Ohio Governor's Residence. Featuring rough limestone walls with smooth-carved stone trim and details, the house has the feel of the picturesque sixteenth- and seventeenth-century English architecture that inspired it. It has twenty-five rooms, twelve bathrooms, and six fireplaces. The recessed front doorway is heavily ornamented, and windows are clustered in stone-trimmed groups. The interior has flagstone floors, large carved fireplace surrounds, handhewn oak ceiling beams, and leaded glass windows. The separate carriage house survives. Former First Lady Hope Taft created a heritage garden behind the residence that features a series of small gardens replicating the major ecosystems found in Ohio.

15-5

15-6

15-5

ST. CHARLES PREPARATORY SCHOOL (ST. CHARLES COLLEGE SEMINARY)

2010 East Broad Street
1924

On the north side of East Broad, St. Charles serves as one of Bexley's gateway buildings. Originally built as a seminary, it now serves as a Catholic high school for boys. This U-shaped structure measures 192 by 170 feet and is three stories in height. Distinctive features include a central tower, arcading along the upper walls of the projecting wings, internal landscaped courtyard, and a single-story arcaded walkway. A basilica-plan chapel was added to the east side of the building in 1940. The building is set back from the street and is reached by a landscaped circular drive.

The campus has expanded and now includes a theater building to the west of the school, a natatorium, and athletic fields to the rear.

15-6

ST. CATHARINE CHURCH

500 South Gould Street
1961
Architect: Edward Ramsey, Columbus

St. Catharine's design is strongly reminiscent of the Art Moderne movement. The church is simple, yet elegant,with its large, plain wall surfaces, geometric decorative treatments, and streamlined metal canopy at the main entrance. Original pastel-colored diamond-pattern stained glass windows have been replaced with newly commissioned windows created by a liturgical artist. The school nearby is even more strongly Art Moderne. Its two colors of brick create a banded effect, and geometric brick piers surmount the school's stone-trimmed entrances.

15-7

15-8

15-7

MILLER HOUSE

385 North Parkview Avenue
1951
Architect: Noverre Musson, Columbus

Two Bexley residences by the Columbus architect Noverre Musson are of considerable interest. Musson designed the Miller House to take advantage of its site on the brink of a steep hill. The building has low one-story brick walls on the driveway side, and the roof has such a low pitch that it is barely visible. In the center of the house, however, a high pyramidal roof dominates the living spaces, with the entire west wall composed of floor-to-ceiling windows. The lower level on this side of the house has open views of the lawn, which slopes steeply to Alum Creek. This home was clearly designed so that there would be a strong relationship between interior and exterior spaces.

15-8

NOVERRE MUSSON HOUSE

2115 Clifton Drive
1967
Architect: Noverre Musson, Columbus

In the architect's own home the proportions are much more vertical than in the Miller House. In addition, Musson used weathered wood shingles for a more highly textured exterior surface. Dominating the interior courtyard entrance is an inverted triangular pediment painted a provocative red. Behind the one-story facade, the main part of the house is two stories high. Its full-wall windows and open balconies take advantage of the wooded site.

16

German Village Historic District

Bounded by Livingston Avenue, Pearl Alley, Thurman Avenue, and Ninth Street

Circa 1840–1910

NR, CR

Today's German Village gives an idea of how most of the south side of Columbus looked in the mid- to late-nineteenth century. In the 1830s German immigrants began settling the area south of Main Street. They held fast to social and religious customs they brought from Germany: several German-language newspapers were based in the area, and Columbus's Maennerchor and Germania clubs began as nineteenth-century German social clubs. St. Mary's Church was one of many churches that conducted services in German. Beer gardens were common, and the breweries just west of the village were all German enterprises.

During World War I both Americanization and anti-German sentiment weakened ties within the German community, and after the war, Prohibition closed the breweries and caused the South Side residents who had worked in them to search for homes near their new jobs. By the 1950s the area was in decline, and by the 1960s city planners began leveling large areas of the South Side in the name of urban renewal and for freeway construction. Local activists, however, saw an area worth saving; they appreciated its narrow streets, small lots, and lack of new development. In the early

1960s they persuaded the city to set aside a 223-acre area under a special design review ordinance. Though German Village preserves only a remnant of what the south side used to be, its cohesion and distinctive allure make it well worth a visit.

The original immigrants brought many of their Old World customs to the new country, but they left their architecture in Germany. There is no truly German architecture in German Village. Nevertheless, much of the Village's charm and character comes from the design, form, and massing of its generally modest buildings, the small lots, the close spacing of the buildings, and the narrow streets and alleys. Other distinctive characteristics include extensive use of brick and stone for buildings, building details, curbs, and sidewalks. German Village has a texture, color, and scale found nowhere else in the city.

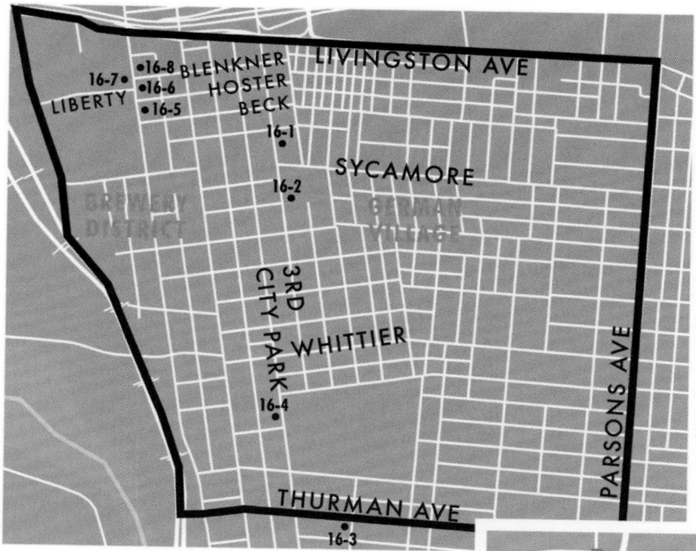

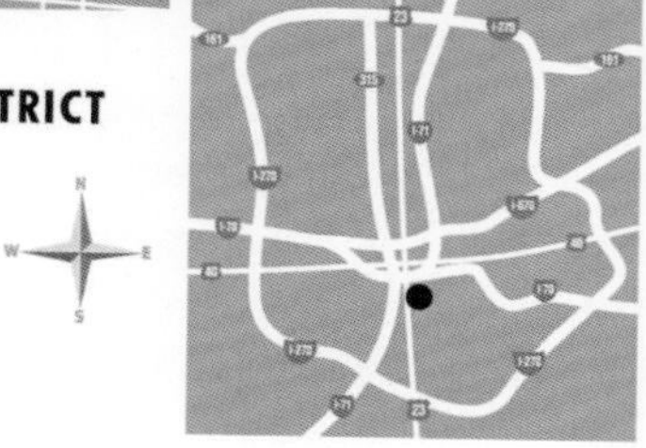

16 GERMAN VILLAGE HISTORIC DISTRICT

16-1 and 16-2

16-1
NR

GOLDEN AGE HOBBY SHOP (THIRD STREET SCHOOL)

630 South Third Street

1864

Italianate

RENOVATION

1976

Architects: Schooley Caldwell Associates

The former Third Street School is one of three nineteenth-century elementary schools in German Village, all of which have survived. Designed in the Italianate style, the building features tall vertical round-arched windows above the entrance; original windows with shaped stone lintels separated by brick pilasters, corbel brickwork, and a bracketed cornice. The main entrance, facing Sycamore Street, was rebuilt in 1925. The limestone surround is inscribed with a quotation from Socrates: "Learning Adorns Riches and Softens Poverty." The building was converted to a new use in the 1970s as the neighborhood's revitalization was firmly underway.

16-2
NR

ST. MARY'S CHURCH

684 South Third Street
1868; spire, 1893
Gothic Revival

AIAC, CLF

RENOVATION
1988
Architects: Feinknopf Macioce Schappa, Columbus

The spire of one of German Village's principal landmarks is visible for blocks around. Buttresses at the side walls and front entrance reinforce the church's powerful Gothic presence. The German character of the church is visible in the restored wall and ceiling murals with their German inscriptions.

Just south of the church and set back from the street is St. Mary's Rectory, an 1872 Italianate building. The rectory's large, round-arched windows with their prominent hoodmolds give the building a strong individual character.

Behind the church and rectory, St. Mary's School, completed in 1887, faces Mohawk Street. While its exterior appearance has been preserved, the school has found a new use as an office building. Its late-Gothic-inspired design complements the church. The Gothic elements include pilasters, a central projecting bay, a pointed-arch main doorway, and cut stone trim.

NEIGHBORHOODS

16-3

16-4

16-3
NR

ENGINE HOUSE NO. 5

121 Thurman Avenue
1895
Richardsonian Romanesque

Although the building is still called Engine House No. 5, its function has changed from putting out fires to housing a popular theme restaurant; today it contains offices. This brick-and-stone building conveys the monumental appearance of the Richardsonian Romanesque style. Its features include a rusticated stone base, large segmental-arched windows with rusticated sandstone surrounds, and a row of round-arched windows separated by short stone columns on the upper floor. Also noteworthy are two reminders of the building's past life: the three-story square hose tower that sits on a battered (sloping inward) stone base and the arched equipment entrances now filled by bay windows.

16-4

STEWART ALTERNATIVE ELEMENTARY SCHOOL (NEW STREET SCHOOLHOUSE)

40 East Stewart
1874
Italianate

This school on the west side of Schiller Park is very similar in overall design to the former Third Street School. Its central entrance, dating from the 1920s, is more pronounced, featuring a stone pediment and rusticated corner quoins. The building exhibits characteristics of the Italianate style, including segmental-arched window openings with carved stone hoodmolds, corbel brickwork in the gable end, and a bracketed cornice. A stone plaque is inscribed "New St. Schoolhouse 1874." It is currently used by Columbus Public Schools as an alternative school.

Brewery District

Both sides of South Front Street between Livingston Avenue and Sycamore Street
1865–1910
CR

Although it was established twenty years earlier, the Brewery District developed primarily in the 1860s. By the early 1870s the big three of Columbus brewing—Nicholas Schlee, Conrad Born, and Louis Hoster—all had large independent breweries. Much of their product was consumed only a few blocks to the east by the mostly German residents of the neighborhood that is today called German Village.

Hoster's brewery occupied a large area at the southwest corner of Livingston Avenue and Front Street, while Schlee's was on the east side of Front Street between Blenkner and Beck. The Germania Club now occupies Schlee's home at 543 South Front, opposite his former brewery buildings. West of Front and south of Schlee's home was Born's brewery, though his bottling works was at Front and Beck.

In 1907 the Gambrinus Brewing Company was built on the northwest corner of Front and Sycamore streets. This brewery operated into the 1970s, when it was demolished. A statue of King Gambrinus, the traditional patron of beer brewers, once graced the main facade of the brewery and is now located a little to the north on the west side of Front Street.

Surviving brewery buildings in this six-block area include malt houses, bottling works, ice houses, stables, and warehouses. Some are quite plain and utilitarian, with massive masonry walls and minimal ornamentation. Others have architectural details common to the period, such as turrets (small corner towers), brackets, and heavy cornices. Brick was the universal building material; cut stone and pressed sheet metal were often used for ornamentation and window trim. Buffeted by national competition and Prohibition, the breweries spent much of the twentieth century as warehouses and factories. Recently, though, life has returned to the Brewery District and to the breweries. Several buildings have been rehabilitated as apartments, offices, restaurants, and stores.

New housing and office construction has replaced some of the earlier buildings. The tallest and most visible is the 500 South Front Street Building.

16-5

16-6

16-5
NR, CR

SCHLEE'S BAVARIAN BREWERY CONDOMINIUMS (SCHLEE'S BAVARIAN BREWERY)

544–560 South Front Street
1875

RENOVATION
Mid-1980s
Architect: Böhm-NBBJ, Columbus

Built in sections, Schlee's brewery has been altered over the years, which accounts for the variation in window openings on the Front Street elevation and the corbeled brickwork and pilasters that appear only in the central section. The upper floors, which were large open spaces with cast-iron columns, have been converted into condominiums, while the rooms in the basement, which were constructed of stone with vaulted ceilings, now have a commercial use.

16-6
NR

SCHLEE MALT HOUSE AND STABLE (BUCHSIEB BLOCK)

526 South Front Street
1883

RENOVATION
Mid-1980s
Architects: Böhm-NBBJ, Columbus

Despite their more recent textured coating, the malt house and stable are largely intact. These brick structures have arched windows and a decorative sheet-metal cornice. Look for a cameo image of Nicholas Schlee just above the first floor level on the facade. Also note the E. C. Buchsieb Block nameplate in the cornice, a tribute to a later owner of the building. A large stable for beer wagon horses behind the malt house is now used as offices.

16-7

16-8

16-7

WORLY BUILDING (HOSTER STABLE)

503 South Front Street
Circa 1880

RENOVATION
1990s

Originally this building housed the delivery horses for the huge Hoster complex on the west side of Front, much of which still stands north of the stable. Note its ornate brickwork and corner towers, which make this former stable one of the featured buildings in the district.

16-8

500 SOUTH FRONT STREET BUILDING

500 South Front Street
1990
Architects: Richard Trott & Partners, Columbus

This building is located among the historic buildings in the Brewery District. Its creative use of brick, steel, and glass creates a three-part facade that looks as if a portion of the building shifted to the north. The main entrance is located within a sheltered recess, while the open steel grid provides a transition to a pedestrian-only environment between this building and its closest neighbor.

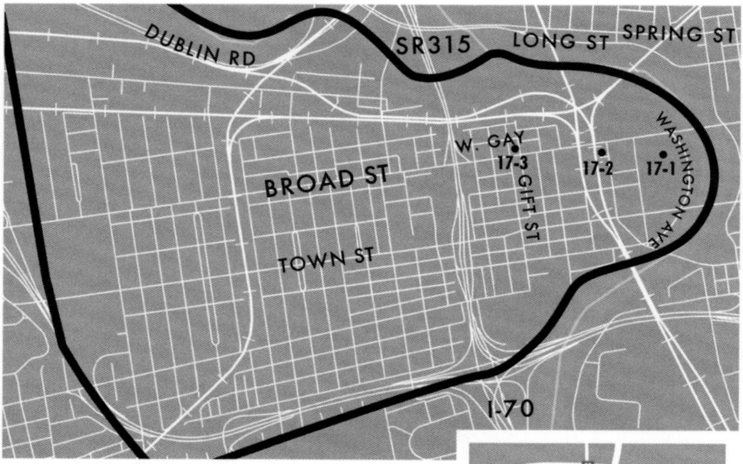

17 FRANKLINTON

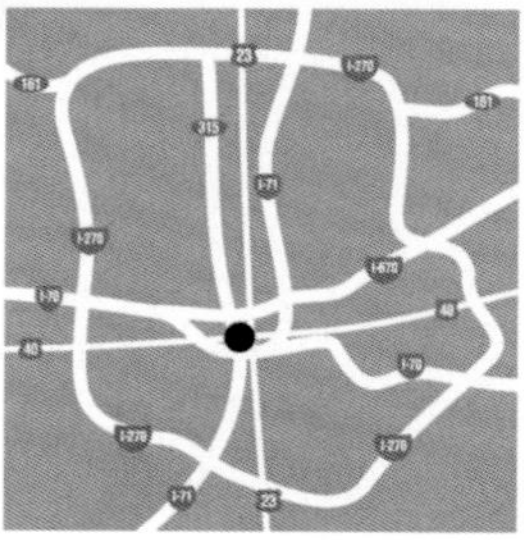

17

Franklinton

Franklinton is the original area of settlement in what would later become the City of Columbus and the state's permanent capital. The land, originally part of the Virginia Military District located between the Scioto and Miami rivers, was used to repay soldiers who had served in the Revolutionary War. Surveyor Lucas Sullivant came upon what appeared to be the perfect site for a town, and in 1797 he developed the community of Franklinton, selling outlying lots for twenty-five cents and choice lots for thirty dollars. Lots on Gift Street were given to those too poor to purchase them. Unfortunately, Franklinton lay on the flood plain between the two rivers, and despite its initial success, frequent flooding restricted its growth until recently, when the completion of the Franklinton floodwall removed this threat.

17-1a

17-1b

17-1
NR, CR

CENTER OF SCIENCE AND INDUSTRY (COSI) (CENTRAL HIGH SCHOOL)

122 South Washington Boulevard
1925
Architect: William B. Ittner, St. Louis

RENOVATION AND EXPANSION
1999
Architects: Arata Isozaki and Associates, Tokyo; NBBJ, Columbus; Moody•Nolan Ltd., Columbus

Situated on a broad curve in the Scioto River opposite downtown Columbus, Central High School was the first building constructed under the Civic Center plan. Its Neoclassical design and strong horizontal lines give it a commanding yet subdued presence on the riverbank.

Designed in an enfolding U-shape, the building has sunken garden areas on both sides of the central entrance walk. The design is restrained; notice how shallow pilasters separate the metal windows. Four fluted Ionic columns mark the main entrance; the entablature above them is inscribed with the building's name. Inscribed elsewhere are names such as Lincoln and Roosevelt, obviously intended to inspire students.

The Center of Science and Industry (COSI) moved to this location in 1999. Japanese architect Arata Isozaki retained much of the original high school facing downtown and created a long elliptical form linked to the school on the west side. The new portion contains the main entrance for the building. Constructed of precast panels, the smooth, gently curved wall surfaces reflect the late-day sun and the blue lights that shine on it at night.

17-2

17-2
NR

TOLEDO & OHIO CENTRAL RAILROAD STATION

379 West Broad Street
1895
Architects: Yost & Packard, Columbus

RENOVATION
1978
Architect: Charles Nitschke, Columbus

One of the city's most whimsical and unusual buildings, the Toledo & Ohio Central Railroad (T&OC) station, like other stations from its era, was designed not only for mundane functions but to delight and impress both customers and the general public. This station served as a passenger depot from 1895 to 1930, when the trains moved to Union Station and the Volunteers of America (VOA) took over the building. The VOA later moved to East Broad Street, and now the City of Columbus owns the property and is committed to its preservation. The T&OC, which connects Toledo and West Virginia, is part of the Norfolk Southern Corporation, and trains still rumble by the station every day.

The station's principal exterior feature is its pagoda-like towers. The central tower, which is just for show, contains no rooms; the carved stone panel on the tower's north side says, "Ohio Central." Dominating the station's interior is a barrel-vaulted waiting room. The vault is composed of wooden ribs and pressed sheet metal panels with plaster bas-reliefs at either end. The original ticket office and window are on the waiting room's west side.

The building lost its original tile roof and suffered much interior damage in a 1975 fire, but the VOA undertook a complete rehabilitation, including restoration of the waiting room.

17-3

17-3

HARRISON HOUSE (JACOB OBERDIER HOUSE)

NR
570 West Broad Street
1807
Federal

SULLIVANT LAND OFFICE

NR, CR
25 North Gift Street
Circa 1820

General William Henry Harrison is thought to have used this building as his headquarters during the War of 1812, but it is also important as an excellent example of early Federal-style architecture. The entrance is especially fine, with a limestone lintel over a paneled recessed entry and an eight-panel door. On the interior, the stairway is a beautiful combination of delicately carved handrails and very thin turned wood balusters. The Franklin County Genealogical Society has offices here.

Originally located at 714 West Gay Street, the Sullivant Land Office was moved to its present site behind the Harrison House in 1986 to preserve it from demolition. This extremely modest—only 9 by 16 feet—brick building sits on a high limestone foundation.

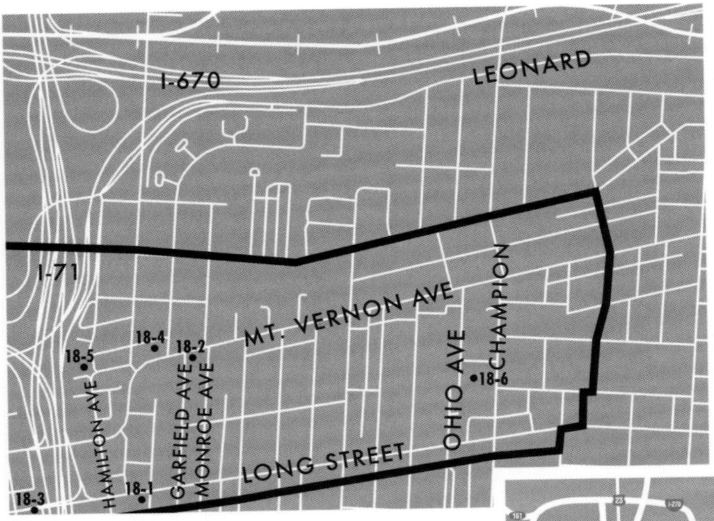

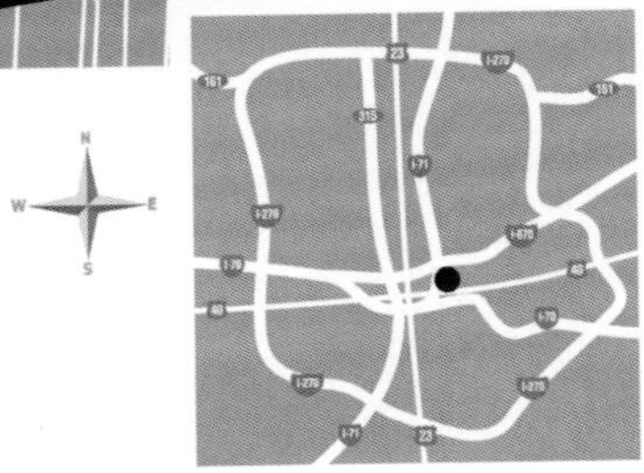

18 MOUNT VERNON AREA

18 Mount Vernon Area

East Long Street and Mount Vernon Avenue

These two streets, lined with late-nineteenth- and early-twentieth-century buildings, served as the center for the city's African American community in the early twentieth century. By the mid-1920s these two streets were thriving with theaters, hotels, restaurants, fraternal organizations, professional offices, and retail businesses owned and operated by African Americans for the benefit of the surrounding neighborhood.

The construction of Interstate 71 compromised East Long Street and severed the connection of Mount Vernon Avenue with downtown, causing considerable urban decline and disinvestment. Renewal efforts began with the construction of Mount Vernon Plaza in the 1970s and received a tremendous boost from the creation of the King Arts Complex. Now new construction is appearing across the street from the Lincoln Theater, new infill housing has been built adjacent to the King Center, and historic homes in the neighborhood are being rehabilitated. There is also a growing appreciation for the area's historical and architectural significance.

18-1

18-1
NR

LINCOLN THEATER (OGDEN THEATER)

777 East Long Street
1928

The Lincoln Theater, built by the Grand Order of Odd Fellows, an African American fraternal organization, was a center of Columbus black culture in the 1930s, '40s, and '50s. Carl Anderson, the builder, was head of an African American construction company in Dayton, and it was managed by the prominent African American entrepreneur Al Jackson. The theater is said to be where the jazz classic "The Jersey Bounce" was written.

It was common for lodge buildings in the late nineteenth and early twentieth centuries to include commercial space; that is why the Lincoln Theater has four commercial storefronts flanking its main entrance. The 6,000-square-foot Ogden Ballroom, later called the Lincoln Club, had a separate entrance.

The theater's exterior design is very spare, with a stripped-down, unornamented look. Smooth stone trim delineates the entrance and storefronts. The upper brick walls have almost no detailing or ornamentation; they rise to parapets, but have no cornices. The windows are simple steel sash with plain stone sills. Inside the 750-seat theater, columns and a decorative plaster cornice were used to create the feeling of an Egyptian palace. A large space to the rear of the stage facilitated the movement of scenery and backdrops.

Steps have been taken to preserve the theater in recent years. The old roof was replaced and the brick exterior restored. The four street-level shop spaces were rehabilitated, and the building has 6,000 square feet of office space on the third floor.

18-2a

18-2b

18-2

NR

Martin Luther King Jr. Performing and Cultural Arts Complex (Pythian Theater and Garfield Elementary School)

867 Mount Vernon Avenue

PYTHIAN THEATER

1926

Architects: Evans & Plato, Louisville

GARFIELD ELEMENTARY SCHOOL

1955

Architects: Brooks & Coddington, Columbus

AIAC, CLF

RENOVATION

1987

Architects: Moody•Nolan Ltd., Columbus

The King Arts Complex, which creatively uses two existing buildings, has become a major cultural institution in the city. Beginning with the rehabilitation of the former Pythian Theater in 1987, the complex expanded into the adjacent mid-twentieth-century Garfield Elementary School in 1989.

The Pythian Theater was built as a fraternal lodge and a theater for the community. It is the only building in Columbus known to be designed by African American architect Samuel Plato of Louisville. Plato was the first African American to receive U.S. Post Office commissions; he ultimately designed forty post offices.

The theater building's rehabilitation combines restoration of historic features with sensitive new construction. Note particularly the columned arcade on the west side. Here the architect created new entrances off a paved plaza to accommodate arriving crowds.

The adjacent school building's arcade of light-colored paired columns visually ties it to the theater building. Although it has a low profile, the building features a tall tower. This building's original colors were those of its construction materials: concrete, metal, and glass. More recently, it acquired a new coat of black paint and new windows. Notice how its exterior marble panels give this building a rich texture. Classes are held in both buildings. The school building also houses the Elijah Pierce Gallery, named after a nationally acclaimed folk artist from Columbus. The complex is located adjacent to a landscaped park.

18-3

18-3
NR

ST. PAUL AME CHURCH

639 East Long Street
1906

St. Paul's remains an extremely active church in the African American community. While its interior follows the symmetrical plan favored in church architecture, its exterior is asymmetrical in design. Two different-sized towers, set far forward, are the main exterior features. Each has a pyramidal roof and brickwork forming arcaded corbel tables, and between them is an arched, stone-trimmed entry porch. The gabled main sanctuary has a large, arched stained-glass window just visible behind the towers. The entire building is set up on a high rock-faced stone foundation. A new health and wellness center being constructed on the west side of the church has substantially increased both its size and the services that are offered.

18-4

18-4

COLUMBUS URBAN LEAGUE

788 Mount Vernon Avenue
1995
Architects: Moody•Nolan, Ltd., Columbus

What appears at first to be yet another new office building proves, on closer inspection, to be a little out of the ordinary. The Columbus Urban League, a non-profit organization devoted to social and economic issues, occupies this headquarters building on Mount Vernon Avenue, not far from Shiloh Baptist Church and the Martin Luther King Jr. Arts Complex.

Constructed of buff brick, the Urban League building has flush windows of dark glass set within rectangular and segmental arched openings. This part of its design is fairly conventional. Not so conventional, however, are the curved east and west elevations, a "break-the-box" design element that seems modest but adds a fair bit of distinction to the composition and creates a visually satisfying building form. Even more unexpected are the large modern renditions of the anthemion, an ornamental element inspired by natural flower or leaf forms that appeared regularly on classical Greek buildings. Its use on modern American office buildings has been less common, but the Urban League building boasts three of them, which rise above the roofline to give the structure an unusual and memorable profile.

18-5

NR

SHILOH BAPTIST CHURCH

720 Mount Vernon Avenue
1923
Late Gothic Revival

ADDITION
2002
Architects: Moody•Nolan Ltd., Columbus

Shiloh Baptist Church traces its roots to 1869, and the current church has been a landmark of the city's African American community for over eight decades. It stands along an isolated section of Mount Vernon Avenue, which together with East Long Street was one of the historic axes of African American life in Columbus. In the 1960s the I-71 freeway just missed destroying the church as it sliced through the neighborhood and disrupted decades-old living patterns. However, the congregation persisted, providing both spiritual and material support to its members. Even today the church operates its own credit union, and the compatible 2002 rear addition was built as an education center for the youth of the neighborhood.

The church was constructed of brick and stone in a late version of the Gothic Revival style, which was inspired in part by the Gothic cathedrals of Europe. The formidable front steps and the asymmetrical square towers give the building a commanding presence. However, the sanctuary, the largest interior space, is an inviting space with a comfortable sense of scale and impressive stained-glass windows. The original east window was the work of the Von Gerichten Art Glass Company, which had studios in both Munich and Columbus; some 850 churches' windows have been credited to this firm. The west window dates from the 1960s.

18-6

18-6

POINDEXTER VILLAGE

East Side of North Ohio Avenue between Mount Vernon Avenue and East Long Street

1937

Art Moderne influences

Poindexter Village was named for the Reverend James M. Poindexter, a prominent local minister, the city's first African American city council member, and a member of the city school board in the late nineteenth century. It is a rare example of public housing that continues to serve its original purpose, as it has done for some seventy years. Poindexter Village was built in farmland acreage outside the settled area of Columbus, an area called the Blackberry Patch. It was one of the first public housing projects built in the United States (Lakeview Terrace in Cleveland, built not long before Poindexter Village, is considered the first).

Unlike many later public housing projects, Poindexter Village was well constructed on a human scale and with some sense of quality; even today its original copper entrance canopies remain in place. Although the residential units were arranged in somewhat regimented rows of connected townhouses, they still created a sense of community and livability. Columbus artist Aminah Robinson, today recognized internationally for her vivid depictions of life in the city, found a major inspiration for her work in her years growing up in Poindexter Village.

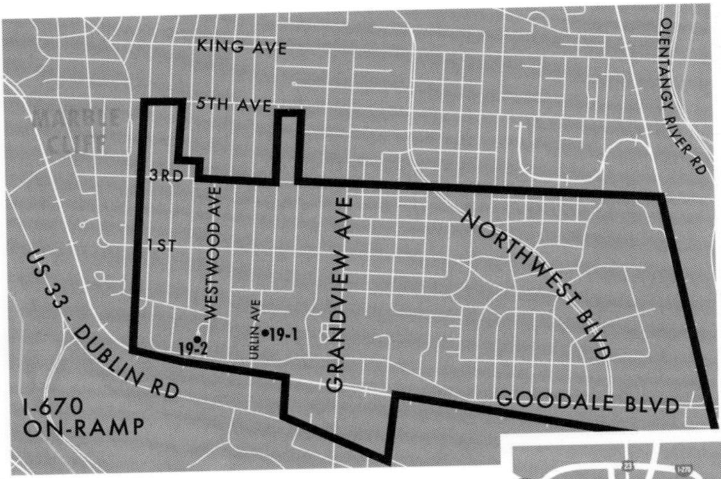

19 GRANDVIEW HEIGHTS & MARBLE CLIFF

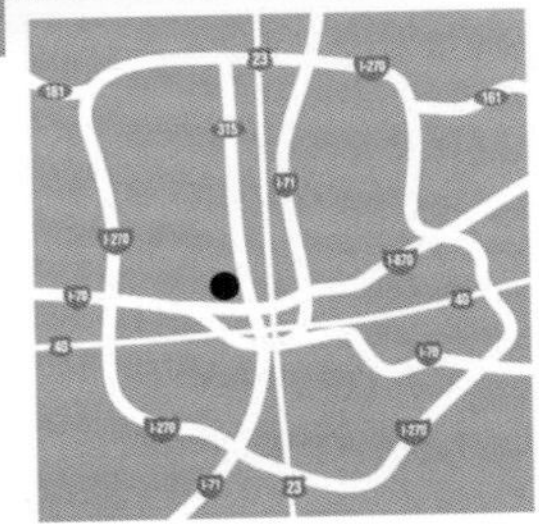

19

Grandview Heights and Marble Cliff

Bounded by Fifth Avenue, Goodale Avenue, and the Scioto and Olentangy Rivers

These side-by-side communities have much of the same appeal as Upper Arlington, Bexley, and some of the city's other close-in suburbs. Both communities are characterized by single-family homes on individual landscaped lots along streets lined with mature trees. Grandview also has a large number of well-constructed, attractively designed apartment houses and busy commercial districts centered along Grandview Avenue and Fifth Avenue. Most structures were built between about 1910 and the 1950s, with some isolated later buildings.

19-1

19-2

19-1
AIAC

SUMMIT CHASE CONDOMINIUMS

1000 Urlin Avenue
1966
Architects: E. A. Glendening & Associates, Cincinnati

Summit Chase claims its place on the skyline because of the pattern of its light-colored balconies, set between projecting brown brick buttresses to provide privacy. Avoiding a regular pattern, the architects placed townhouse units at random, giving this high-rise building an eye-catching design visible from a great distance. From its hillside site above the Scioto River valley, the Summit Chase offers unencumbered, sweeping views of downtown.

19-2
AIAO, AIAC

STONEGATE VILLAGE

Bluff and Westwood Avenues
1989
Architects: Acock Schlegel, Columbus

Continuing in the tradition of close-in Columbus suburbs such as Old Arlington and Bexley, Stonegate Village has picturesque European revival building forms, styles, and materials. By subtle manipulation of scale and use of a village-like street pattern, Stonegate Village creates a unique sense of place. The meandering pavement, stone walls, steeply pitched gable roofs, stone and stucco, and multipaned windows all combine to create a richness of texture and a sense of visual quality. In the 1920s Bexley's Sessions Village pioneered this type of development in Columbus.

20
Upper Arlington

Upper Arlington Historic District

Bounded by the Scioto River, Andover Road, West Fifth Avenue, Cambridge Boulevard, and Riverside Drive
NR

New Upper Arlington

North of Upper Arlington Historic District, bounded by Henderson Road and North Star and Kenny Roads

In 1913 developers King and Ben Thompson bought nearly 1,000 acres of farmland on the Scioto River northwest of downtown Columbus. This land's location, topography, and physical environments made it the perfect place for their new community, Upper Arlington.

The Thompsons began their upscale development in a 500-acre area located southward from Lane Avenue to Fifth Avenue and eastward from the Scioto River to Northwest Boulevard. In addition to planting many trees in Old Arlington, the developers established separate commercial and residential sections. William Chase Pitkin Jr., a Cleveland landscape architect, did the landscape plan for the new community. He was known for his work on country estates and college campuses as well as Kingswood Center in Mansfield, Ohio.

Old Arlington consists of more than 1,100 buildings, most of them single-family residences. Less than 1 percent are commercial and less than 8 percent are multifamily. For many buildings contractors used stone from nearby Marble Cliff quarries. Brick and stone building materials, curvilinear streets, and landscaping attest to the care with which the Thompsons developed the community's picturesque suburban character.

King and Ben Thompson showed how much faith they had in Old Arlington by building their own homes there. King Thompson's, built in 1915, is at 1930 Cambridge Boulevard; it is noted for its green tile gable roof. Old Arlington structures date from about 1915 to 1935 and represent a full palette of twentieth-century revival styles. Executed in stone, Old Arlington's commercial center on Arlington Avenue at Guilford Road has the feeling of a European village.

20 UPPER ARLINGTON

20-1

20-2

20-1

UPPER ARLINGTON MUNICIPAL SERVICES CENTER

3600 Tremont Avenue
1971
Architects: Schooley Cornelius Associates, Columbus

Located on a prominent site at the intersection of Tremont Avenue and Kenny Road, this contemporary stone building is horizontal in form, with a copper roofline. The textured stonework on the center's exterior is carried through to interior spaces, forming the walls of the entrance lobby and city council chambers. The plaza area, with a geometric freestanding clock tower, is reminiscent of more traditional public spaces.

20-2

ST. MARK'S EPISCOPAL CHURCH

2151 Dorset Road
1957
Architects: Brooks & Coddington, Columbus

AIAC

ADDITIONS
1988
Architects: Phillip Markwood Architects, Columbus

St. Mark's tiled gable roof and overall form are strongly reminiscent of St. Stephen's, adjacent to the OSU campus. Unlike St. Stephen's, however, St. Mark's facade is a solid masonry wall without windows or ornamentation. Its other end wall is composed of vertically proportioned panels set into a metal grid framework and turns inward toward the other structures in the complex.

A tall, stylized structural steel tower in the center of the site serves as an updated version of the traditional steeple. Around it, ancillary structures make up the complex. A canopy with an undulating roofline supported by slender columns links one such building with the main church. Drawing the entire complex together is a long wall whose surface is patterned with both closed and open square elements, a pattern that is carried over into part of a building wall. Mounded lawn areas and large shade trees complete the site and provide a contrast to the light-colored planes and angles of the buildings.

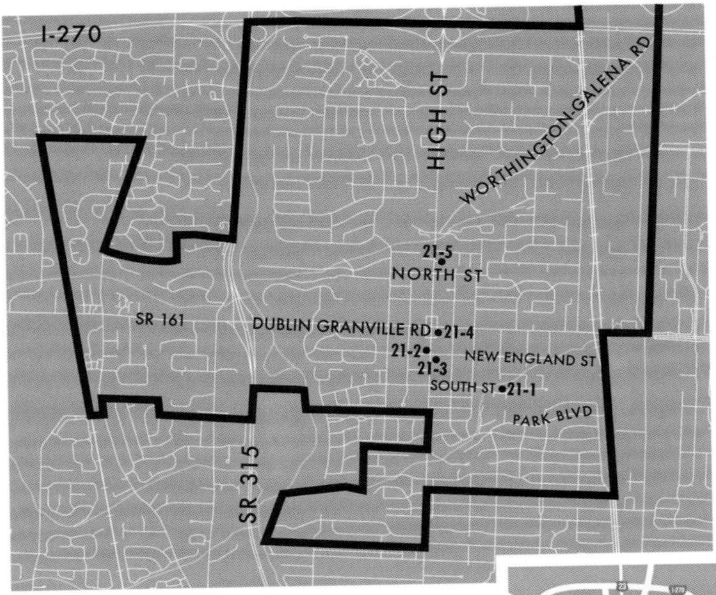

21 WORTHINGTON

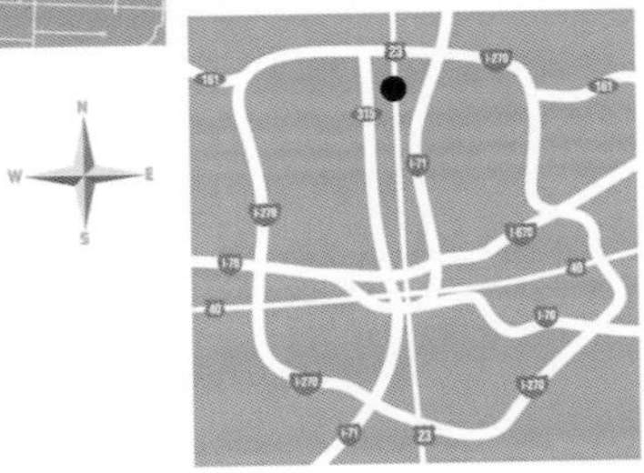

21 Worthington

Established in 1803 by settlers from Connecticut, the physical form of Worthington still reflects its New England roots. The Village Green, which is listed in the National Register of Historic Places, is at the center of the plan and is still the heart of the community. Located at the intersection of High Street and Dublin-Granville Road, it is surrounded by an orderly grid pattern of streets. Churches and public buildings are located on the Green with a historic commercial district along High Street. The residential area of Old Worthington, bounded by North, South, Morning, and Evening streets, reflects the architectural diversity of a community that evolved over 200 years.

Worthington has long been concerned about its historic architecture, and a number of early nineteenth-century buildings remain. But history is only part of the story; Worthington is also home to Rush Creek Village, a nationally recognized mid-twentieth-century residential neighborhood inspired by the work of Frank Lloyd Wright.

21-1a

21-1b

21-1
NR

RUSH CREEK VILLAGE

East end of South Street
1950s
Designer: Theodore Van Fossen

Southeast of the original plat of Worthington, Rush Creek is a community of single-family homes built primarily in the 1950s. Frank Lloyd Wright's influence on Theodore Van Fossen's work is evident in the Rush Creek designs. The developer, Richard Wakefield, also designed and built his own home on the north side of the Rush Creek Village entrance. The houses tend to be low in profile and carefully designed to take advantage of their sites' natural features. Inspired by Wright's Usonian houses, many of these houses are quite small, yet they are masterpieces of efficient design, with built-in storage and furniture to maximize the use of space. Although modest building materials such as Roman brick, concrete block, poured concrete, and wood were used, the buildings are each unique and blend effortlessly into their natural environment.

Several homes that appear to be only one story from the street extend downhill to the rear for two or even three floors. Despite rather close spacing, it is nearly impossible to see one house from the next.

In recognition of its significance in the fields of architecture, landscape architecture, and planning, Rush Creek was listed in the National Register of Historic Places before the normally required fifty years of age. While it is attractive at any time of year, the best time to view Rush Creek is in the winter, when both the buildings and the topography of the sites are visible. Architect Rich Pontius designed a house on the last remaining lot at 559 White Oak Place overlooking Rush Creek.

21-2

21-3

21-2

WORTHINGTON INN (HOTEL CENTRAL)

649 High Street
Circa 1833; 1850s; 1880s

A landmark in downtown Worthington, the Worthington Inn was originally a two-story stagecoach stop where lodging cost twenty-five cents a night, and a beef stew dinner, a dime. Only the front section dates from around 1833; the inn was enlarged in the 1850s and 1880s. Following a 1901 fire, the owner added a third-floor ballroom and mansard roof, as well as the circular fire escape and porches you see today. The building underwent a major renovation in 1982 and was a successful inn. While the restaurant remains open, the hotel portion has closed for conversion to condominiums.

21-3
NR

NEW ENGLAND LODGE

634 High Street
1820
Federal

ADDITION
1957
Architects: Sims, Cornelius & Schooley, Columbus

Located across the street from the Worthington Inn, the New England Lodge is the oldest Masonic temple west of the Allegheny Mountains. This fine Federal-style brick building has an extremely unusual arched panel on the facade, into which the doors and windows are set. The arch is said to symbolically represent Freemasonry. Notice especially the outstanding gabled pediment, which has dentils on all three sides. In the middle is an arched niche containing Masonic symbols. The building received a large brick addition in 1957.

21-4

21-5

21-4
NR

ST. JOHN'S EPISCOPAL CHURCH

700 High Street
1831
Early Gothic Revival

ADDITION
Architect: Charles Nitschke, Columbus

North of the New England Lodge is the oldest church in Franklin County, St. John's Episcopal Church. Though the building dates from 1831, the congregation organized in Worthington in 1804, shortly after the original settlers arrived. The stone for the church's foundation came from Rush Creek and the Olentangy River. Take note of this church's simplicity: its doors and windows are pointed arches and its roof is a stepped gable. Its square central tower is topped by a short frame tower with corner spires.

21-5
NR

ORANGE JOHNSON HOUSE

956 High Street
Circa 1816–30
Federal

RENOVATION
1972
Architect: Gilbert Coddington, Columbus

The Orange Johnson House, one of the finest historic homes in the Columbus area, is located north of the Village Green. Its original owner was a Connecticut comb maker who moved to Worthington in 1814 and constructed the rear portion of the house. As he became more successful, he added the five-bay Federal section along High Street. The building is notable for its well-executed arched entry with delicate fanlight and sidelights, interior woodwork, and main staircase. In the 1970s the Worthington Historical Society hired Gilbert Coddington to restore this house, which is now a museum.

Gems

22
Gems

Several buildings worthy of mention in an architecture guide to Columbus are located outside the areas already identified. They represent a wide range of building types, dates of construction, and architectural styles, but all contribute to the character of the built environment in central Ohio.

22-1a

GEMS

22-1b

22-1

GREEN LAWN CEMETERY

1000 Greenlawn Avenue
1848
Architect: Howard Daniels, Cincinnati

CHAPEL

1902
Architect: Frank L. Packard, Columbus

Originally, Green Lawn Cemetery was an 83-acre site east of Harrisburg Pike (State Route 3), south of West Mound Street. Today the cemetery covers more than 340 landscaped acres. Howard Daniels, the original designer, was perhaps best known for his design of the superb Greek Revival Montgomery County Courthouse, built in Dayton between 1845 and 1850.

Many names from the city's earliest years can be found among the tombs and stones at Green Lawn: Sullivant, Starling, Sessions, Johnson, Goodale, Deshler, Hayden, and Battelle. The numerous family mausoleums have considerable architectural merit. Their designs include Greek Revival, Gothic Revival, Neoclassical, and Romanesque Revival styles.

Most imposing, however, is the Neoclassical Revival style of Packard's chapel. Built entirely of marble, the chapel features a recessed entrance with Ionic columns in antis. The building's windows are stained glass, and its central dome is leaded glass. The mosaic murals are from the Tiffany Studios in New York City. Today the chapel serves as a mausoleum. Packard is said to have designed his own tomb, one of several Neo-Egyptian Revival-style tombs.

22-2

22-2
NR

OLD PORT COLUMBUS AIRPORT TERMINAL AND CONTROL TOWER

4920 East Fifth Avenue
1929
Architects: Allied Architects Association, Columbus
Art Moderne

Shortly after World War I, city officials began lobbying for an airport near Columbus. Ten years later, armed with an $850,000 bond issue, the city built a new airport it advertised as "The World's Greatest Air Harbor." The airport and terminal building opened in July of 1929.

At that time Port Columbus was the first transfer point for East Coast passengers traveling straight through to the West Coast. They traveled by train at night and by airplane during the day, transferring to planes in Columbus after an overnight train ride. When Port Columbus was opened, the entire trip from coast to coast took forty-eight hours, but only two years later planes were flying transcontinental passengers the entire distance.

In the southeast corner of today's Port Columbus, the first airport terminal has been preserved and small private aircraft still use its original runway pattern.

The two-story, rectangular, boxy brick terminal has a three-story tower at its northwest corner. Its very simple Streamlined or Art Moderne design features minimal ornamentation—black glazed bricks set among the buff-colored bricks in the walls. Vertical columns support the octagonal tower with its sheet metal pyramidal roof. Later additions were removed and the building was rehabilitated for use as private offices.

22-3

22-3

PONTIFICAL COLLEGE JOSEPHINUM

7625 North High Street
1931
Architects: F. A. Ludewig Company, St. Louis

CLF

RENOVATION
1989
Architects: Feinknopf Macioce Schappa, Columbus

North of Worthington, the Pontifical College Josephinum dominates the now suburban skyline. This is the only Catholic educational facility in the United States under the direct jurisdiction of the Pope. Reverend Joseph Jessing originally founded this seminary in 1888 on Main Street near downtown Columbus.

The main building at the Josephinum complex is brick with a local limestone foundation. It reveals Late Gothic Revival–style influences, such as smooth brick walls with stone trim for sills and belt courses. The main building is symmetrical in plan and features a tall two-stage central tower. Pinnacled turrets rise from the buttressed lower stage. The complex contains four chapels, each featuring liturgical art through paintings, statuary and architecture. St. Turibius Chapel, the largest, was renovated in 1989.

22-4

22-4

SOUTH SIDE SETTLEMENT HOUSE

310 East Innis Avenue

1980

Architects: Studio Works, Venice, California; Feinknopf Macioce Schappa, Columbus

The South Side Settlement House is a facility providing social services to the surrounding South Side community. Its design is unique for its time. The building mass is broken up into a series of smaller connected structures positioned around a formal central courtyard. The courtyard design includes wall surfaces enlivened by the use of contrasting concrete block in a striped pattern, an innovative use of galvanized tubing as columns, and a monumental staircase created by Columbus sculptor John Sunami. The building maintains the scale of the residential neighborhood where it is located.

22-5

22-6

22-5
AIAO, AIAC

ST. MARGARET OF CORTONA CHURCH

1600 North Hague Avenue
1969
Architects: Pietro Belluschi, Boston; Brubaker/Brandt, Columbus

St. Margaret's is built of stone from the nearby Marble Cliff quarries. Traditionally, Italian quarry workers were members of this parish, and the church's design and materials acknowledge that link. The rough texture of the exterior is carried through to the interior walls.

The interior plan is purposely unregimented, with seating for 300 arranged to encourage people to sit around the altar, not just in front of it. High above, a powerful network of wood roof beams rises and opens into a light tower that floods the altar with natural light.

To make people feel at ease, the church is without ornamentation and is small and intimate in scale. Even the entry vestibule has an angled design intended to cause people to meet and mingle.

The church received an honor award from the National Conference on Religious Architecture in 1970.

22-6

ONLINE COMPUTER LIBRARY CENTER (MIDVO BUILDING)

500 Post Road, Dublin
1970
Architects: Perkins & Will, Chicago

Located in the suburban community of Dublin, the Online Computer Library Center (OCLC) is designed to wrap around an artificial lake so that the important interior spaces have a view of the water. The building's maximum height is two stories, with the first floor deeply recessed on the west wing, The exterior's dark metal, tinted glass, and aggregate panels combine with its entirely flat roof to give the structure a long, low profile and a feeling of repose.

Glossary of Architectural Terms

ABUTMENT: Supporting column for an arch.

ANTHEMION: Ornament based on the honeysuckle flower and leaves, as in classical architecture.

APSE: The semicircular or polygonal altar end of a church.

ARCADE: A blind or open range of arches with their pier or column supports.

ARCH: A means of spanning an opening by the use of small units, usually masonry; described by its shape as round (semicircle), lancet (tall and pointed), or segmental (segment of a circle).

ASHLAR: Rectangular large units of dressed masonry.

ASYMMETRICAL: Not identical on both sides of a central line.

ATRIUM: An open central court.

BALUSTRADE: A series of balusters supporting a railing.

BARREL VAULT: Also known as a tunnel vault. It is semicircular in cross-section and similar to a barrel cut lengthwise.

BASILICA: Early Christian church form in which the central nave is taller than the side aisles. Clerestory windows and an apse may also be present.

BAS-RELIEF: The slight projection of forms or figures from a flat background.

BATTER: To slope inward; a wall that slopes inward as it rises is said to be battered.

BATTLEMENT: A parapet having large indentations or slots; also known as crenellation.

BAY: One structural module or unit of a building; a building can be described as being so many bays wide by so many bays deep.

BAY WINDOW: A projecting section containing windows and supported by a foundation.

BEDFORD LIMESTONE: Also called Indiana limestone; can be cut and carved into a variety of shapes and sizes.

BELLCAST: Shape having a flare like a bell. The term can be applied to a roof or eaves.

BELT COURSE: A horizontal band, often of contrasting masonry, around a building; also called a stringcourse.

BELVEDERE: Small open-sided or enclosed structure on a rooftop designed for viewing the scenery.

BRACKET: A projecting element that supports a cantilevered section, such as a cornice.

BUNDLED TUBE: A structural framing system employed by Skidmore Owings & Merrill in the 1970s to allow design of skyscrapers with a more open floor plan.

BUTTRESS: An engaged pier designed to strengthen a wall.

CAMPANILE: A freestanding bell tower.

CANTILEVER: A projecting beam, overhang, or upper floor.

CAPITAL: The uppermost part of a column or other support.

CASEMENT WINDOW: A window that has a vertical sash hinged to swing outward.

CASTELLATED: Having battlements.

CHERUB: Sculpture of a chubby naked baby, sometimes used as decorative accents for facades; also known by the Italian term *putto.*

CLAD: Covering or protective coating.

CLERESTORY: An upper glazed portion of a building designed to provide natural light at or near the top of interior spaces.

COFFER: A recessed ceiling panel; the ceiling is said to be coffered.

COLONNADE: A row of columns carrying an entablature.

COLUMN: A vertical support, usually round and normally having three parts: base, shaft, and capital.

CONICAL: Cone-shaped.

CORBEL: A support produced by extending successive units, usually masonry, out from a wall surface; a range of corbeled masonry, often arcaded, is a corbel table.

CORINTHIAN COLUMN: A slender fluted column having an ornate bell-shaped capital decorated with acanthus leaves.

CORNICE: The top section of a classical entablature; also the projecting terminus of a wall.

CRENELLATION: *See* Battlement.

CROCKET: A blunt, usually masonry, ornament terminating a spire or pinnacle.

CURVILINEAR: Having curved lines.

CUT STONE: Building stone that is cut to a specific size so that it will fit into a designated location on the building's facade.

CUPOLA: A small domed structure surmounting a roof.

DENTIL: One of a row of small rectangular blocks forming a molding below a cornice; a cornice having this molding is denticular.

DORIC COLUMN: A heavy, fluted column having no base and a plain, saucer-shaped capital.

DORMER: A vertical window projecting out of a sloping roof.

EAVE: Section of a roof that projects over an exterior wall.

ENGAGED: Used to describe a column or pier attached to or partially embedded in a wall.

ENTABLATURE: The construction above the classical column capital, consisting of architrave, frieze, and cornice.

FACADE: The front or face of a building.

FLEMISH BOND: A brick pattern in which headers and stretchers are laid alternately so that each header is centered on the stretcher above and below it.

FREESTONE: A soft stone that can be cut easily, such as limestone or sandstone.

FRIEZE: The middle section of an entablature, often decorated.

GABLE ROOF: The common inverted V-shaped roof; the triangular upper part of the wall end of such a roof is a gable; a miniature version used decoratively is a gablet.

GAMBREL ROOF: A double-sloped roof.

GARGOYLE: Grotesque carvings of animals or people that decorate primarily Gothic-inspired architecture.

HALF TIMBER: Method of timber framing in which the spaces between timbers are filled by plaster or masonry.

HAMMERBEAM: A cantilevered interior beam used to support structural members above it.

HEADER: A brick laid with its end exposed.

HIPPED ROOF: A roof having a slope on all four sides; the line of meeting of two of these slopes is a hip.

HOODMOLD: A projecting, usually decorative, molding over a window or door.

IONIC COLUMN: A fluted column having two scroll-like ornaments in the capital.

KEYSTONE: The top member of an arch.

LANCET ARCH: A narrow pointed arch.

LANTERN: A structure with windows built on a roof or dome.

LINTEL: A beam supported at each end by a vertical post—the most common method of spanning an opening.

MANSARD ROOF: A roof having two pitches, the lower one nearly vertical and the upper nearly horizontal.

MOSAICS: Small pieces of tile arranged in a bedding material to form a pattern or picture.

MULLION: A vertical divider in a series of windows.

NAVE: The section of a church where the public worships.

ORIEL: A projecting section containing windows and supported on corbels or brackets.

ORNATE: Elaborately decorated.

PAGODA: Buddhist temple multistory tower; usually a memorial or a shrine.

PARAPET: A low protective wall at the edge of a roof.

PEDIMENT: A triangular or segmental-curved gable.

PERGOLA: Open wood frame structure with a double row of columns or posts connected by beams and covered with vines or climbing plants creating a garden walk.

PIER: A vertical supporting member.

PILASTER: An engaged column or pier, attached to a wall surface.

PINNACLE: The tall, tapering pyramidal or conical termination of a tower or other feature.

PROSCENIUM ARCH: In a theater, the area between the curtain and the orchestra.

PORTE COCHERE: A roofed structure extending from the entrance of a building over an adjacent driveway and sheltering those getting in or out of vehicles.

PORTICO: A pedimented porch supported by columns.

POST-TENSIONING: A method of strengthening cast concrete by means of applying tension to reinforcing rods after the concrete has hardened.

PRECAST CONCRETE: Concrete cast in the form of a structural element, such as a panel or beam, before being placed in final position.

PYRAMIDAL: Taking the shape of a pyramid with a square base and sides sloping to join at the top.

QUOIN: Masonry treatment at the corners of a building or at window and door openings that contrasts with the rest of the walls.

QUONSET HUT: Prefabricated structure with a semicylindrical roof made of corrugated metal. This inexpensive portable building was developed for use by the Armed Forces.

RAFTERS: Structural element that supports the covering for a roof.

REINFORCED CONCRETE: Concrete with metal rods inserted into it to give it tensile strength.

ROCK-FACED: Stone having an undressed, natural-appearing surface.

ROSE WINDOW: A circular church window having decorative tracery.

RUBBLE: Undressed, broken stone used in building.

RUSTICATION: Decorative stonework with emphasized joints.

SANDSTONE: A sedimentary rock;like limestone, which can easily be cut and carved.

SASH: The usually operable part of a window or door that holds the glass or lights; described by its method of operation as 6/6 (six lights over six lights), double-hung (sliding vertically), casement (hinged at one side), and so on.

SCAGLIOLA: An imitation or ornamental marble consisting of finely ground gypsum mixed with glue.

SEGMENTAL ARCH: An arch that is less than a semicircle.

SHAFT: The section of a classical column between the base and the capital.

SILL: The horizontal member located at the top of the foundation and supporting the structure above it; also the horizontal member at the bottom of an opening.

SPANDREL: The areas between arches in an arcade; the nonstructural exterior infill between floors in multistory frame construction, usually in opaque glass.

STRATIGRAPHIC: Related to geological layers of rock.

SYMMETRICAL: Divisible into equal parts; a regular repeated pattern.

TERRA-COTTA: Decorative molded and fired clay units.

TRACERY: Fancy or curving stone window mullions.

TREFOIL: An architectural form having the appearance of a three-part leaf.

TRIUMVIRATE: A group or set of three.

TURRET: A small, often corbeled tower located at the corner of a building.

VAULT: A space roofed by an arched structure. A barrel vault is an arched semicircular ceiling, like half a barrel. A groin vault is produced by the intersection of two barrel vaults.

VERNACULAR: Architecture that uses common local materials and forms.

WAINSCOT: A decorative treatment, often of wood, given the lower part of interior walls; also called a dado.

WING WALL: A subordinate wall usually built to support an abutment.

Index

References are to identification numbers of guidebook entries (chapter number-item number). A reference noted as "0" (e.g., 9-0) is to a description at the beginning of a chapter.